Shri Sai Baba's
Teachings and Philosophy

Born in Baroda (Gujarat) on 29 October 1918, Lt Col. Mukundrao Balvantrao Nimbalkar (Retd) graduated with English and Marathi literature in 1939 and joined Baroda State Army as cadet officer. In 1949, he was enlisted in the Indian Army and served first in the Maratha Regiment and then in the Fourth Gorkha Rifles. He retired in 1968 as Lieutenant Colonel after 29 years of service.

A year before retirement, while recouping at the Naval Hospital at Bombay from a heart ailment, he chanced to read the Life of Sai Baba by N. V. Gunaji. On discharge from the hospital, he read the book once again, and on 3 August 1967, had a miraculous chance to touch and pay respects to the silver sandals of Sai Baba being taken from Shirdi to London. Since then his lifestyle underwent a total transformation.

Being well-versed in Sanskrit, he studied the Ramayana, the Mahabharata, the Gita, the Upanishad and the Vedas. He also studied the Marathi Jnaneshvari, Eknath Bhagavat, Tukaram Gatha and Das Bodh, all considered to be the four Vedas of Maharashtra. From 1980, he started contributing articles, in both Marathi and English, to Shri Sai Leela. In 1993, he published a profusely illustrated, voluminous book in Marathi Shri Sainche Satya Charitra, in prose form with detailed commentary and notes from the original Shri Sai Satcharita.

Sterling Books on : Sri Shirdi Sai Baba

Published by
Sterling Publishers Pvt. Ltd.

Shri Sai Baba's
Teachings and Philosophy

Lt Col. M. B. Nimbalkar (Retd)

New Dawn

NEW DAWN
a division of Sterling Publishers (P) Ltd.
A-59 Okhla Industrial Area, Phase-II,
New Delhi-110020.
Tel: 6916165, 6916209, 6912677, 6910050
Fax: 91-11-6331241
E-mail: ghai@nde.vsnl.net.in
www.sterlingpublishers.com

Shri Sai Baba's Teachings and Philosophy
© 2001, M. B. Nimbalkar
ISBN 81 207 2364 3
Reprint 2002

Published by Sterling Publishers Pvt. Ltd., New Delhi-110016.
Lasertypeset by Vikas Compographics, New Delhi-110029.
Printed at Shagun Composer, New Delhi-110029.

CONTENTS

CONTENTS

PREFACE

"Like the holy waters of the Ganges, this *Shri Sai Satcharita* purifies others through moral excellence. Blessed are the ears of the listeners (or the eyes of the readers) of this *Sai Satcharita* which is the means of success in this life as well as the life after death." (21)

"If this *Sai Satcharita* is compared to nectar (drink of the Gods), is the nectar sweeter than *Sai Satcharita*? Nectar will only protect one from death, but *Sai Satcharita* will save one from taking births again and again." (22)

—*Chapter 13*

From the above stanzas, it will be realised how invaluable is *Shri Sai Satcharita* written by the late Shri Govind Raghunath Dabholkar alias Hemadpant. In it, the teachings of Shri Sai Baba, in his own words and in the words of Hemadpant, are spread over at various places. Some Sai devotees have collected and published them in *Shri Sai Leela* and other books. But unless they are sorted out subjectwise, it is difficult for anybody to properly understand them and bring them into practice. I firmly believe that any teachings contained in a book are fruitful only if they are properly understood and brought in action.

"Reading only is not sufficient. It must be brought into action, otherwise it will be wasted like water poured on an inverted pot." (72)

—*Chapter 21*

I, therefore, thought that if Sai Baba's teachings were selected and collated subjectwise, they would be very useful. Fortunately, at the very time, I came across a series of booklets, viz, Money, Food, Sleep, etc, containing teachings of Shri Aurobindo and the Mother of Pondicherry, and I thought of writing, if not a booklet, at least an article on each subject of Sai Baba's teachings and philosophy.

Accordingly, I started writing such articles, and with Sai Baba's grace published 21 such articles in *Shri Sai Leela* (English) — the official periodical of Shri Sai Baba Sansthan, Shirdi — from July-August 1993 to November-December 1995.

Now they are being published as a book by my younger brother, Jaisinh, as a humble service to the Sai devotees. I am, indeed, very grateful to him.

— M. B. Nimbalkar*

---

* The author since expired on 24 August, 1998, after a brief illness. Mr Jaisinh Nimbalkar did a lot of work and published the first draft which was corrected and approved by the late author. However, the book could not be published by him due to extraneous reasons. The book is now published by Sterling Publishers Pvt. Ltd, New Delhi, under the guidance of Mr S K Ghai, an ardent Sai devotee.

WEALTH

Sai Baba's advice, regarding wealth or money, to his devotees, is found everywhere in *Shri Sai Satcharita*. When we see the growing tendency among people to amass wealth day and night, by any means fair or foul, the truth of Sai Baba's constant preaching in this regard seems to be convincing. These persons believe that by wealth alone can all pleasures and happiness in the world be theirs and that their progeny will be rolling in wealth forever. But if they were to seriously think for a moment, they would realise that they are not really happy. Their minds are uneasy due to constant worries and their bodies are troubled with frequent diseases. They cannot even have a good night's sleep. Yet their greed for more and more money never ceases.

Sai Baba has given appropriate advice to those seeking self-realisation and to those leading a normal, mundane life where wealth is concerned.

For Those Seeking Self-realisation

Sai Baba's advice is that self-realisation is impossible unless one gives up greed for wealth. Chapters 16 and 17 of *Shri Sai Satcharita* reveal the story of a visitor seeking from Baba the knowledge of *Brahman* (the cause and the essence of the universe). Finding that this rich but miserly visitor could not think of lending even five rupees to Baba in spite of possessing a bundle of notes worth Rs. 250/- in his pocket, Baba told him: "*Brahman* (the cause and essence of the universe) has a permanent enmity with avarice. Where there is avarice, there is no place for meditation. How then can you aim for real liberation or renunciation? Avaricious persons also become neglectful of prescribed rites and usages." (69)

"On account of avarice there is no peace, no satisfaction nor freedom from anxiety. With avarice in mind, all accomplishments towards emancipation already achieved, are wasted." (70)

— Chapter 17

"Remember that one who has great yearning for money can never achieve self-realisation." (165)

"If while listening to the knowledge of the Supreme Spirit, one is thinking of sense-objects and worrying of worldly business, then self-realisation will also be not that full." (166)

— Chapter 16

Mhalsapati was Baba's very close and dear devotee. On account of poverty, he maintained his family with great difficulty. He watched Sai Baba daily distributing hundreds of rupees but he never begged Baba to give him some. When a rich person named Hansraj wanted to give some cash in Baba's presence to Mhalsapati, he refused it and Baba did not tell Mhalsapati to accept it.

Baba said : "My devotee will never be attracted towards money and will not be caught in the grandeur of wealth." (71)

— Chapter 36

Chapter 29 reveals this fact about a lady from Madras who used to get visions of Shri Ram very often, but on account of her greed for money these visions had stopped.

On arriving at Shirdi and Shri Sai Baba remembering her previous spiritual status, not only gave her vision of Shri Ram again but also transformed her husband into a devotee.

When Kaka Mahajani's boss Dharmasi Thakersy came to Shirdi, how beautiful was the advice Baba gave to him! "There was a person whose house was full of grains and money but his mind was always uneasy and full of worries. He had no disease physical or mental but he always liked to get involved in any uncalled for work." (115)

"He used to wander listlessly here and there carrying heavy loads on his head without any reason. He would keep it down and lift it again. He had no peace of mind." (116)

"I told him 'Why are you wandering like this?' Sit down quietly in one place."

— *Chapter 35*

Sai Baba used to advise his rich devotees not to waste their money in gratification of senses but to use it for some good cause. "Wealth will be of use to wealthy persons only through charity. The fruits of charity only lead to real spiritual knowledge." (132)

"This wealth, acquired through hard labour, people unnecessarily spend on favourite enjoyments instead of on accumulation of charity benefits." (133)

"One who does not waste his crores of rupees worth wealth acquired by collecting each pice in his fancy for sense enjoyments, is a happy person." (134)

— *Chapter 35*

That is why Sai Baba got the dilapidated Shani Temple repaired through Gopalrao Gund, inspired Rao Bahadur Sathe and Kakasaheb Dixit to construct buildings for visiting devotees to stay in, and the wealthy Bapusaheb Butty to construct the Samadhi Mandir for Sai Baba's samadhi. In the case of Nanasaheb Chandorkar, Baba had sought his help much earlier. Nanasaheb, with his money and official status, used to arrange accommodation for visitors in tents and settled loans that Sai Baba took for arranging accommodation and food for visitors.

Thus Baba, by repressing the rich devotees' ego of official status and wealth, led them slowly towards the spiritual path, as if he wanted to say : "Do not forget that opulence is temporary like the afternoon shadow, hence do not unnecessarily harass anybody on account of intoxication of wealth." (71)

- *Chapter 32* of *Bhakta Leelamrit* by Das Ganu Maharaj

To those poor and penniless amongst seekers of self-realisation, Baba has permanently assured: "There will be no shortage of food and clothes at the residence of my devotees." (33)

— *Chapter 6*

"Those who worship Me exclusively and serve Me always with a mind full of reverence, I consider it my promise to look after their livelihood and protection." (34)

— *Chapter 6*

For Those Leading a Secular Life

For such devotees Sai Baba stressed that one should be content with whatever money one got through honest efforts. One should not get agitated and distressed over it and should never adopt means involving immorality, killing or bribes, because one has to bear the consequences of these bad deeds, if not in this life then in the future lives. In this respect Baba has given a beautiful example to Nanasaheb Chandorkar, "A clerk kills his proprietor and becomes the de facto owner." (12)

"After becoming the owner, the clerk leads a life of comfort and luxury. He moves in horse-drawn carriages and says he is now happy." (13)

"By killing his proprietor, he has in fact acquired a sin which will either become stock acquired through the good and evil actions of the present and other particular births, or the actions of the present life with reference to its merits and demerits and subsequent pleasure and pain to be experienced in births yet to be." (14)

— *Chapter 33* of *Bhakta Leelamrit* by Das Ganu Maharaj

In Chapter 46 of *Shri Sai Satcharita*, Sai Baba, while narrating previous life-stories of two she-goats, has described how they were two brothers first loving each other immensely and afterwards, for the greed of money, killing each other and as a result were reborn as she-goats. Similarly in Chapter 47, Sai Baba, while describing the three previous births of a serpent and a frog, says: "Similarly, listen attentively, in this story, to how extreme greed for wealth leads to one's downfall." (15)

"In that also the tendency towards enmity is never good. Always control your mind from it, otherwise it will utterly ruin your life." (31)

— *Chapter 47*

On account of right efforts or by luck if one gets money, one should certainly enjoy it. But at the same time one should also make others, especially the poor and needy persons, participate in one's enjoyment. Sai Baba advised: "Respect the guests. Lord Shri Krishna will be pleased if you offer water to the thirsty, food to the hungry, clothes and verandah to the homeless." (74)

— *Chapter 19*

That is why probably in Chapter 24, Baba, while joking with Annasaheb Dabholkar on account of roasted grams found in the folds of his coat sleeves, advised everybody that eating without sharing was not good.

Similarly, Baba has condemned any miserly person who neither enjoys the money himself nor allows others to enjoy it: "Shame! Shame to one who is miserly in spite of possessing immeasurable wealth. He experiences disgust and weariness all his life." (30)

— *Chapter 40*

But any charity (almsgiving, building temples, etc) is worthwhile if only given voluntarily. A charity given under pressure from somebody else or for the sake of fame is useless. Sai Baba says in this connection : "God does not like anything given without love, out of force and fear, on being earnestly pressed or on being caught in a difficult situation. He immensely likes anything little also, if given with love and sincerity." (101)

"One who will give without sincerity, his giving will be worth nothing. He will experience without delay that in the end it will bear no fruit." (109)

— *Chapter 47*

On the subject of almsgiving, Baba's following advice is worth noting: "In case you do not wish to give any money or alms to anybody, do not give it, but do not shout at him angrily and act like a dog." (143)

— *Chapter 19*

At the same time, Baba impressed upon those leading a mundane life the necessity of money for the maintenance of the family and therefore to use it carefully and frugally: "Constant over-generousness is also not good. Once whatever money one possesses is finished, nobody cares for you afterwards." (79)

"Remember! One should indulge in charities (almsgiving, building temples, etc) according to one's income only and never overspend by borrowing money for the same." (72)

"While giving money in alms, one should consider thoroughly its necessity as well as the suitability of the receiver and then only give liberally."

— *Chapter 72* of *Bhakta Leelamrit*
by Das Ganu Maharaj

Sai Baba's Own Example

Sai Baba gave different but proper advice regarding money to those seeking self-realisation and to those leading a secular life. However his advice was not just a show of words but preaching after practice. For instance, his renunciation of all sensuous delight and gratification is well known. He used to live in the open under a neem tree or in the dilapidated *masjid* or *chavadi*. His dress was a patched, long robe and a piece of cloth tied on the head. His seat was a torn piece of sack cloth only. For food he used to beg around in the village. What better renunciation could there be than this?

Later on, as Sai Baba's fame spread far and wide, devotees started pouring in great numbers. Some ardent devotees prepared a seat with soft cushions, decorated him with ornaments of diamonds and pearls and cast around his body embroidered silk shawls but Baba had no fascination for these. On the contrary, many a time he used to pull them out and throw them away in anger. For the *chavadi* procession, devotees brought a palanquin but Baba never sat in it. During meal-time, varieties of food were brought as offerings but Baba hardly tasted them and distributed them amongst all the devotees present. Similarly, every day hundreds of rupees worth cash would be collected as a gift to Baba, but he never kept a single rupee for himself. Instead he would distribute all the money thus received so that by the evening nothing was left with him.

However, this generosity was for charity only and that too for the needy only. For other everyday transactions like purchasing grains and condiments for cooking food for the needy, Baba used to haggle a lot with the shopkeeper over the price in order to avoid being cheated. But at the same time, he never used to accept free service from anybody. Whether a potter providing earthen pots for watering flowerbeds or hawker women selling fruits or a boy just bringing a ladder for Baba to climb on the roof of a house, Baba's payment was prompt and on the spot.

Finally, if we summarise the teachings of Baba in matters of money, his following words are quite noteworthy: "Poverty is the real kingship — much superior to nobility. Allah is the friend of the poor." (68)

— Chapter 5

$$\boxed{2}$$

FOOD

Sai Baba's teachings have given great jolts to those who observed rigid customs and beliefs. His teachings, especially those about food, were quite revolutionary and reformatory, but of course very correct and truly beneficial.

Non-vegetarian Food

In Hindu and Jain/Buddha religions especially, there is a belief that unless one gives up eating non-vegetarian food, one cannot attain emancipation or knowledge of the Supreme Spirit. Sai Baba himself was an emancipated soul and had full knowledge of the Supreme Spirit and was capable of giving such experiences to others. However, he not only had no objection to non-vegetarian food, but never insisted that his devotees should give it up. In his early days he used to cook non-vegetarian food himself in a big pot and after consecrating it through a moulvi by reciting the *fatiha,* used to send as *prasad* to Mhalsapati and Tatya Kote Patil before distributing it to others. (*Chapter 38*)

There might be two reasons for this. One could be that Sai Baba, with his mission of achieving unity amongst Hindus and Muslims, wore a Muslim fakir type of dress and lived like a fakir. Hence, accepting non-vegetarian food was quite appropriate. Secondly if we carefully consider the teachings of our scriptures, it will be clear that denial of non-vegetarian food is only one of the means to attain emancipation or knowledge of the Supreme Spirit and not a goal in itself. Most of the famous *suktas* in the *Vedas* have been authored by *kshatriya* (warrior caste) sages such as Vishwamitra. Similarly kings like Janaka, who was famous as a Brahma-jnani (knower of the Supreme Spirit), were also of warrior castes, and non-vegetarian food was not taboo for them. To give this up, to avoid killing of innocent animals for the sake of one's enjoyment of tasty food or because non-vegetarian food becomes a hindrance in achieving concentration of mind during meditation by increasing attributes of passion (*Rajo guna*) and ignorance (*Tamo-guna*), is of course commendable. But to say that without avoiding non-vegetarian food one cannot achieve emancipation or knowledge of the Supreme Spirit is not correct. Otherwise great seers like Mohammed (*Paigamber*) and Jesus Christ, would not have been born at all. Moreover, in India, those who do not take non-vegetarian food do so because they believe in the principle of non-injury, or because they fear that the attributes of passions and ignorance would increase.

They are vegetarians because it is customary in their castes for generations not to eat meat. These persons have never tasted non-vegetarian food and hence they have disgust or aversion for such food. Nowadays, young men and women of these castes enjoy it in restaurants and hotels. Similarly, amongst those having vegetarian food also, fried items full of spices and difficult-to-digest sweets, although adhering to the principle of non-injury, do tend to increase attributes of passion and ignorance, which are obstacles for concentration in meditation.

In fact, as a person progresses in his *sadhana*, his attraction for non-vegetarian and rich food dwindles down and is ultimately lost permanently. Just because one gives up eating meat, fish and eggs as a result of attending *bhajan-melas* or visiting temples in old age, one does not attain eminence amongst the *sadhakas*. One may give up non-vegetarian food but such vegetarianism is useless if one gets emotionally upset or tempted by rich food, or if one does not hesitate to rob or cheat a person in business dealings, or if one ill-treats cows, buffalos and birds.

Sai Baba's ideas must have been on the same lines probably. That is why he never advised his devotees to give up eating meat. Sometimes jokingly (as in Chapter 38), he used to ask an orthodox brahmin like Dada Kelkar to go and buy mutton from the market, or (as in Chapter 23) order his great brahmin devotee Kakasaheb Dixit to kill a goat with a knife. But this was only to test their readiness to execute whatever order was given by him, their Guru, and therefore before the person started acting, he used to stop them. Similarly he never tempted or encouraged his vegetarian devotees to eat non-vegetarian food.

Baba's method of persuading his devotees from abstinence of non-vegetarian food was quite different and unique. He used to tell his devotees every now and then that he was present in every creature moving about. He said to Mrs Tarkhad (Chapter 9), "The dog which you saw before meals and to which you gave the piece of bread is one with Me, so also the other creatures (cats, pigs, flies, cows, etc) are one with Me. I am roaming in their forms. He who sees Me in all these creatures is My beloved. So abandon the sense of duality and distinction and serve Me as you did today."

Once, one is thoroughly convinced of this idea, who will dare to eat non-vegetarian food? Will it not be given up automatically? Thus, Sai Baba also preached 'non-violence' in food, but in a very realistic, practical and tactful manner.

Onions

What applies to non-vegetarian food also applies to onions. Sai Baba himself used to eat onions with bread daily and did not like anybody expressing disgust towards it or not eating it because of its bad smell. Incidents of his teasing and ridiculing Dada Kelkar, Das Ganu and Kusha Bhau are well-known. He once surprised a student of yoga by eating bread and onion in front of him and later gave a proof to him of his super yogic powers, as if he wanted to tell people that because of baseless customs and beliefs, one was depriving oneself of onion and garlic which are greatly praised by the *Ayurveda* (Indian Medical Science) and are excellent health-giving foods. Isn't the poor and hard- working farmer able to perform the laborious task of ploughing his field by eating bread and onion only? If a person faints, a crushed onion is the quickest and simplest first aid in the far-off villages. Recently, the Western countries, after research, have declared garlic as an excellent cure for heart disease and high blood pressure and since then we Indians have started buying costly tablets (Lasona) containing the essence of garlic.

Fasting

Another important advice of Sai Baba concerning food was that of fasting. Sai Baba never kept a fast himself, nor did he allow others to do so. Mrs Gokhale wanted to keep a fast for three days at Shirdi (Chapter 32) but Baba asked her to go to Dada Kelkar's house to cook as Kaka's wife was in menses and not permitted by custom to cook. Further, he not only ordered her to feed Kaka and his family members with sumptuous and delicious *puran polies* (sweet stuffed breads) but asked her to eat to her heart's content by giving up the fast. Baba used to say: "The mind of the person fasting is never at ease, then how could it attain the *Paramartha* (goal of life)? God is not attained on an empty stomach; first the soul has to be appeased. In short, when all organs get their proper nutrition and are sound, we can practise devotion and other *sadhanas* to attain God. Therefore, neither fasting nor over-eating is good. Moderation in diet is really wholesome both for the body and mind."

— Chapter 32 pp. 177, 178

Baba persuaded Mrs Radhabai Deshmukh who was determined to remain without food and water unto death so long as Baba did not give her the *Updesh Mantra*, to give it up by narrating his own experience with his Guru. He explained to her the simplest method of achieving oneness with God: "You look at ME and I look at you."

— Chapter 19

The Sanskrit word for fasting is 'उप+वास' which means 'seat near'. Since fasting is done for religious purposes, it means seating near God. In other words, on that day one has to think and act with a pure mind and meditate on God's form but we hardly do this. On the contrary, since we continue to attend to our normal secular business and other duties on that day, we also continue to indulge in immoral activities such as telling lies, cheating others, etc. There are many methods of observing fast, as narrated in our religious books. But at present the following methods are in vogue:

i) To accept only fruits and milk, avoiding meals both at daytime and night.

ii) To accept only fruits and milk by day and eat a meal after sunset.

iii) To eat a meal once at daytime and accept only fruits and milk at night.

But do we observe these also correctly? Whatever you eat during fasting days must be in small quantities. The idea is to give rest to our digestive system. But instead, what do we do? Fruits we hardly eat. But other so-called 'permitted' items we eat in full and a number of times. One meal also which we eat is not only overeaten but is also extra rich. The result is indigestion. Thus there is neither any religious nor health benefit. Sai Baba probably had realised this and that is why he stopped his devotees from observing such fasts in the name of religion.

Not Disregarding Offers of Food

Sai Baba advised that during meal time, do not go out on an empty stomach disregarding any offer of food. On the contrary, it should be regarded as an auspicious sign of success. To do any job perfectly, one requires energy which can only be acquired by eating food. Secondly, refusing something offered by somebody lovingly, means hurting his feelings which is certainly not a done thing. Sai Baba narrates his own experience as to how he and his companions lost their way in the woods because they disregarded the *banjarin's* offer of food and guidance (Chapter 32). However, later, when Sai Baba accepted the *banjarin's* food and guidance, he was able to carry out the quest successfully. Similarly, Appasaheb Kulkarni was not able to find the fakir when he rushed out of his home in a hurry without his meals (Chapter 33). However, after taking his meals, he strolled out with his friend, and the fakir himself was seen approaching him and demanding *dakshina*.

Never Eat Anything without Sharing with Others

In Chapter 24, Sai Baba has conveyed this principle very effectively by making fun of Anna Saheb Dabholkar, the author of *Shri Sai Satcharita*, when some grains of gram were seen stuck in the folds of his coat sleeve. Sai Baba further explained that when no person or animal is present nearby, one should offer it to Baba by remembering him. This will result in the devotee avoiding food which is impure and not fit to be enjoyed not only in the sense of taste only but in all senses also.

To illustrate this, Hemadpant (in the same chapter) has narrated the story of Sudama, a co-student of Shri Krishna and Balram in the *ashram* of their Guru Sandipani. Once when they were collecting firewood in the forest, Krishna was thirsty and asked for some water. Sudama advised him not to drink water without eating something. Shri Krishna, therefore, rested his head on Sudama's lap and slept. After sometime, he woke up and heard Sudama chewing something. He asked Sudama what he was eating. But Sudama, although he was eating grams, lied to Shri Krishna saying that he was not eating anything, but that his teeth were chattering due to cold. Later as a result of this, Sudama, although a chum of Lord Krishna, had to pass his life in utter poverty. However, he later offered Shri Krishna a handful of parched rice earned by his wife with her own labour. Shri Krishna was pleased and gave him a golden mansion to live in and enjoy life.

Baba himself never ate anything without sharing it with others. Everyday he used to go out begging and whatever food was collected, he used to place it in the earthen bowl in the masjid. Some beggars used to pinch 3-4 bread slices and dogs and birds used to eat out of it, but Baba never drove them away. Whenever any devotee offered him fruits and richly cooked food, he hardly tasted it and distributed it amongst the devotees present. Every afternoon in the Dwarkamai, when the meal was served and ready to eat,

Baba would call out for Bade Baba (a fakir from Malegaon) and make him sit next to him on his left respectfully as an honoured guest. Then after the meal, Baba used to pay him Rs. 50 as *dakshina* and walk with him 100 paces to see him off.

In the *Taithirya Upanishad, Anuvak* II, it is stated 'अतिथि देवो भव' (May the guest be to thee, a God).

In the *Bhagavad Gita* also Shri Krishna, in Chapter 3 says,

यज्ञशिष्टाशिनः सन्तो मुच्यन्ते सर्वकिल्बिषैः ।
भुञ्जते ते त्वघं पापा ये पचन्त्यात्कारणात् ।।13।।

(The virtuous who partake of what is left after sacrifice, are absolved of all sins. The sinful ones who only cook and eat for themselves eat only sins.) Thus Sai Baba very effectively taught this principle of not partaking of any food without sharing with others, both by precept and example.

'अतिथि' (guest) literally means 'without date'. Hence a guest in the above context should mean one who appears unexpectedly and stays not more than one day. In today's state of towering prices and food rationing, therefore, this meaning would have to be borne in mind to ensure that an unwanted and persisting person does not take advantage of our generous nature.

Charity of Food

Last but an important advice about food given by Baba is about charity: "Different *sadhanas* (means of accomplishments) are prescribed in our scriptures for different ages. *Tapa* (penance) is recommended for *Krita* Age, *Jnana* (knowledge) for *Treta* Age, *Yajna* (Sacrifice) for *Dwapara* Age and *Dana* (Charity) for *Kali* (Present) Age. Of all the kinds of charities, giving food is the best one. We are much perturbed when we get no food at noon. Other beings feel similarly under similar circumstances. Knowing this, he who gives food to the poor and hungry is the best donor or charitable person. The *Taittiriya Upanishad* says, "Food is Brahma, from food all the creatures are born and having been born, by food they live and having departed, into food they again enter." Other kinds of charities, viz, giving away wealth, property, clothes, etc, require some discrimination, but in the matter of food, no such consideration is necessary. Let anybody come to our door at noon, he should be served food and if, crippled, blind and diseased come, they should be fed first and the able-bodied persons and our relatives afterwards."

— *Chapter 38, pp. 208-209*

We remember how Sai Baba expressed his great pleasure when Mrs Tarkhad fed a hungry dog during her meal-time (Chapter 9). He further said, "Ever act like this and this will stand you in good stead. First give bread to the hungry and then eat yourself." (p. 55)

Similarly, we know what Baba said to Laxmi Bai Shinde, who was annoyed because Baba gave the bread and vegetables urgently cooked for Baba, to a nearby dog, "Why do you grieve for nothing? The appeasement of the dog's hunger is the same as Mine. Though some speak and others are dumb, the hunger of all creatures is the same. Know for certain that he who feeds the hungry, really serves ME with food." (Chapter 42, p. 233)

In this regard also, Baba himself had set an example. In early days, he very often used to feed the poor and helpless by himself cooking food in big pots (*handi*). He used to buy the grains and spices from the bazaar and do the needful grinding also by himself. Later, devotees started thronging to Shirdi in large numbers, and cooked food in the form of *naivedya* in large quantities, so there was no need for Baba to cook. However, he never stopped distributing this *naivedya* food to all and sundry. He himself hardly tasted it.

Conclusion

Sai Baba was always practical and realistic in his advice. While eulogising on charity, he also warned about overdoing it and becoming a debtor (*Bhakti Leelamrit*, ch. 32, by Das Ganu Maharaj). The crux of his advice regarding food was to learn to be satisfied with whatever food was served. This would not only ensure good health but would also help one in one's efforts for attaining emancipation.

3

SPEECH

"**I** shall consider you blessed when you will renounce all attachments, conquer lust and palate: and getting rid of all impediments, serve God wholeheartedly and resort to the begging bowl (accept *Sanyas*)." (Chapter 44, p. 239)

The above is the reply given by Sai Baba to Bapusaheb Jog who asked him why even after serving Baba for so many years, his mind was not calm and composed and why he failed in his efforts for self-realisation. Sai Baba always laid stress on controlling pleasures of the senses, especially those of the sexual organ and the tongue. About sexual pleasures, we will discuss the subject in a later chapter. The tongue however has two functions — to taste the food and to speak. About tasting the food we have already discussed it previously and in the following let us see what Baba's teaching was about speech.

Use of Scornful and Slightful Speech

In our scriptures, great stress is laid on 'non-violence' which means not to hurt anybody physically, mentally or by speech. Sai Baba had realised that of all the above, harsh and scornful words hurt a person much more than physical or mental violence. Such cutting words are not easily forgotten and cannot be withdrawn also. Consequently they cause everlasting ill-feeling. Sai Baba, therefore, not only advised his devotees, "Not to speak cuttingly to anyone so as to hurt him to the quick" (ch. 19, p. 104), but also, said: "Let anybody speak hundreds of things against you, do not resent by giving any bitter reply. If you always tolerate such things, you will certainly be happy" (ch. 19, pp. 101-102), and to make sure that they did follow his advice, he said, "He who carps and cavils at others, pierces Me in the heart and injures Me but he that suffers and endures, pleases Me most." (Chapter 44, p. 237)

Arguments and Disputes

Regarding control of the tongue, another advice by Sai Baba was to avoid arguments or hot discussions on any subject with others. Arguments spring from egoism. Arguments lead to quarrels and spread enmity. We remember how, in Chapter 2, Dabholkar, on the very first day of his visit to Shirdi, had a heated discussion with Balasaheb Bhate regarding the necessity of having a Guru (a spiritual teacher or preceptor) and how Baba checked Dabholkar's argumentative habit permanently by addressing him as 'HEMADPANT' (corrupted form of Hemadripant, a well-known and learned minister of the Yadav kings, Mahadev and Ramdev, in the 13th century).

Indulgence in Scandal-mongering and Discussions of Others' Affairs

Sai Baba advised his devotees not to indulge in scandal-mongering or slandering of others. For this, he had his own methods of correcting the defaulters. Being omniscient, he knew when and where the devotees had committed the fault and so he could correct them effectively by taunting them. Sai Baba pointed out a pig to such a defaulter and said to him, "Behold how with what relish it is gorging dung. Your conduct is similar. You go on reviling your own brother to your heart's contents" (Chapter 19). Needless to say that the devotee was ashamed and took the lesson to his heart forever.

Similarly (Chapter 21) a pleader from Pandharpur had unnecessarily taken part in a discussion in the bar-room regarding the sub-judge Noolkar's coming and staying at Shirdi for cure of his ill-health. When the pleader himself arrived at Shirdi, Sai Baba said, "How cunning people are! They fall at the feet, offer *dakshina*, but inwardly give abuses behind the back. Is not this wonderful?" The pleader understood that the remark was aimed at himself, and being convinced, later said to Kakasaheb Dixit, "This is not a rebuke to me but a favour and advice that I should not indulge in any scandal or slander of others and not interfere unnecessarily in others' affairs."

Always tell the Truth

In our scriptures, repeated stress is laid on always speaking the truth. Our national motto is 'सत्यमेव जयते' (Truth only succeeds). In the *Mahabharata*, we have heard of Dharmaraj, the eldest amongst the Pandavas, who always spoke the truth, but once in his life he told a lie and therefore had to spend a few hours in hell. Sai Baba was always practical and realistic in his teachings. He never told his devotees in words not to tell a lie and always speak the truth. But the devotees knew that Sai Baba was अंतर्ज्ञानी (knower of the secrets of every being's heart) and would certainly catch them if they told a lie. Hence they dared not speak untruth in his presence. Hemadpant in his original Marathi *Shri Sai Satcharita* rightly says:

असत्य चालेना साईंप्रती । असत्ये नाहीं साईंची प्राप्ति
असत्ये जाणै अधौगति। अति दुर्गती असत्ये ।। 138 ।।

(Untruth does not work before Sai and Sai cannot be
procured with untruth. Untruth means downfall. Untruth
in the end takes you to hell.)

खोटे सांगनि भागेना काज । साई महाराज सर्वसाक्षी ।। 49 ।।

(Success is not possible by telling a lie, Sai Baba is omniscient.)

However, there are some instances in Sai Baba's life,
where he himself has told lies. He wanted to give Ramdasi's
Vishnu Sahasranama (a book giving a thousand names of
Vishnu and held second in importance to the *Bhagavad Gita*)
to his devotee Shama for initiating him in its recitation. So
he called Ramdasi and told him a lie that he was suffering
from intense stomach-pain and asked him to go to the bazaar
to fetch some *sonamukhi* (a mild purgative drug). When
Ramdasi went to the bazaar Sai Baba rose from his seat,
picked up the copy of *Vishnu Sahasranama* and gave it to
Shama who was not willing to take it (Chapter 27). Similarly,
getting the *udi* and *arati* urgently for the safe delivery of
Nanasaheb Chandorkar's daughter at Jamner, Sai Baba
himself took the form of a tonga-driver and told a lie to
Bapugir that the tonga and the refreshment were sent by
Nanasaheb Chandorkar from Jamner (Chapter 33).

Now, how do we interpret such acts? Firstly, the saints
do not have to bear the consequences of these acts, whether
good or bad, since they do not claim the doership of these
acts to themselves. Secondly, even if such acts are sinful, the
saints are prepared to bear their consequences for the sake
of their devotees. In the first instance, Sai Baba wanted to
favour his devotee Shama with some religious practice and
hence he enacted this drama. Normal advice by words would

not have been that effective. In the second instance, Sai Baba wanted to respond to Nanasaheb Chandorkar's fervent prayers to save the life of his pregnant daughter Mainatai who was having severe labour pains and was unable to deliver at Jamner. In this case, there was urgency to reach the *udi* and *arati* more than 100 miles away and that too at night. Hence, Baba not only prompted Bapugir to go to his native place at that odd hour but helped him to reach Jamner from Jalgaon railway station in a tonga resorting to lies to convince Bapugir. Thus, saints would do anything to favour their devotees or to help them in their calamities. Haven't we heard of a number of instances where saints have taken on themselves serious and painful diseases of their devotees and suffered them willingly? Sai Baba himself had taken on himself four fully developed bubos of Dadasaheb Khaparde's young son and suffered them willingly (Chapter 7). How then would saints ever hesitate to perform sinful acts for the sake of their devotees and suffer the consequences, if any?

Telling the truth — nothing but the truth — sometimes becomes problematic in everyday life. Nowadays there is a shortage of coins. While travelling in a bus or rickshaw, the conductor or the rickshaw driver always demands the exact amount, saying he has no change. Now even if we have the change, we would need it for the return journey. Therefore we are tempted to tell a lie, since telling the conductor or rickshaw driver that we need the change for the return journey will not work; telling the truth will end in serious difficulties on our return journey. Actually the conductor or the rickshaw driver himself many times bluffs that he has no change. So what should we do? Follow the principle of 'सत्यं वद' (Tell the truth always).

Another instance is our grandson's asking for blank papers for drawing pictures. Normally once or twice we can always spare. But when our stock is coming to an end, what do we tell them? If we give away every paper from our stock, there is the problem of going all the way to the market in old age to fetch them. If we tell the grandson that there is no paper left with us, we transgress the principle of truth. Then how should we act?

From the above discussion, personally my views are as follows. One must always speak the truth. Never tell a lie, at least not for one's own self-interest. However, sometimes for the benefit of others there is no harm in telling a little lie. For example, if telling some sad news is likely to shock a person, there is no harm in telling a lie that such a thing has not happened or that we do not know about it. Similarly, if somebody has offered some food with love and care and even if it is not relished by us, will it not be wiser to praise the quality of the food smilingly rather than bluntly telling the truth and hurting the feelings of the person! Such acts are even supported by our scriptures:

सत्यस्य वचनं श्रेय : सत्यादपि हितं वदेत ।
यम्दूत हितम त्यंनतमेतत्सत्यं मतं मम!

– महाभारत शातिपर्व

(Telling the truth is good but telling what is beneficial to others is better. In my opinion what results in the ultimate welfare of all beings is real truth.)

सत्यं ब्रयात् प्रियं ब्रयात् न बऋयात् सत्यमप्रियम् ।।134।।

मनुष्मृति अ.4

(One should speak the truth and speak what is pleasing and agreeable to others. Never speak the truth which is not pleasing and agreeable to others.)

Always Keep Your Promise

Sai Baba preached that if you promise anything to anybody you must fulfil it. Never make a false promise. Devotees normally pray and make a vow to their deity or Guru to do some act or offer something on condition that their desires be fulfilled, but once fulfilled they forget to fulfil their vow. There are many instances where Sai Baba prompted such devotees to fulfil their pending vows. For instance, Appasaheb Kulkarni wished to pay Rs. 10 to the fakir who had visited his residence during his absence, and Baba got it fulfilled by approaching him again and demanding the full amount (Chapter 33). Similarly we have read how Sai Baba manoeuvred to get Shama's long-pending offering to Sapta Shingi Goddess fulfilled (Chapter 30). Sai Baba was highly pleased to note his devotee Cholkar giving up sugar and also drinking tea without sugar until his vow to offer sugar candy to Sai Baba by visiting Shirdi was fulfilled (Chapter 15).

Talk Less

Sai Baba himself followed this principle of talking less. He never gave long lectures but gave his devotees suitable experiences by narrating suitable stories. For spiritual advancement, observing silence for some time every day is good. Baba himself practised this by spending some time twice a day in Lendi Baug till the end of his life regularly. Talking too much consumes a lot of energy, hence even in day-to-day business, it is advisable to avoid unnecessary talk.

Repeat God's Name

In speech, Sai Baba's most important advice was about repeating God's name. He himself used to repeat 'Allah Malik hai' (God is Lord) constantly. He was fond of making others chant God's name continuously day and night for a whole week. This is known as *Nama-Saptaha*.

Hemadpant also adds : "The efficacy of God's name is well-known. It saves us from all sins and bad tendencies, frees us from the cycle of births and deaths. There is no easier *sadhana* than this. It is the best purifier of our mind. It requires no paraphernalia and no restrictions. It is so easy and effective." (Chapter 27, p. 145)

Summary
In short Sai Baba's advice on speech was as follows:

a) Not to speak cuttingly to anyone so as to hurt him to the quick. On the contrary one should bear the other person's outburst calmly.

b) Avoid arguments and disputes.

c) Never indulge in scandal-mongering or ridiculing others.

d) Always speak the truth.

e) Speak soft and sweet words.

f) Keep your promises.

g) Talk less and observe silence frequently.

h) Repeat God's name as often as possible.

4

BHAKTI MARG

There are four methods of obtaining God-realisation
— *Jnana* (knowledge), *Yoga* (control of mind), *Karma*
(selfless work) and *Bhakti* (love of God). Sai Baba himself
had achieved full knowledge of *Brahman* or the Supreme
Being. He was also known to be a great *yogi* having
supernatural powers. He also seems to have practised
rigorous penance and indulged in selfless work all his life.
But to his devotees, Sai Baba normally advised the method
of *Bhakti* or love of God. This method of knowledge is the
quickest but it is very difficult and there is a chance of failure
due to conceit. In the *Yoga* method, the body and the mind
have to be strained greatly and quite a few restrictions are
to be observed in intake of food and drink. In the *Karma*
method, a common man finds it difficult to give up doership
and fruits of his actions. However, the method of love of
God is different. It is the easiest of all and can be conveniently
followed by all even while leading a secular life. That is
why Sai Baba repeatedly advised his devotees to follow the
Bhakti marga or love of God.

In Chapter 6 of *Shri Sai Satcharita*, Hemadpant quotes
Sai Baba's words: "Four paths, viz. of *Karma, Jnana, Yoga*
and *Bhakti* lead us separately to God. Of these, the path of
Bhakti, although thorny and full of pits and ditches, is
without diversions. If you, relying on your *Sadguru*, avoid

pits and thorns and walk straight, it will take you to your destination (God)." (Chapter 6, p. 31)

What is Bhakti?

Bhakti means love of God. Sage Shandilya in his *Shandilya Bhakti Sutra,* says while defining *Bhakti* 'सा परानुरक्तिरीश्वरे' (It is devoted attachment or love to God). Similarly Sage Narada in his *Narada Bhakti Sutra* defines *Bhakti* as 'तस्मिन् परमप्रेमरूपा' (It is exceeding and the highest love of God).

In *Shri Sai Satcharita* also Hemadpant talks about *Bhakti* as follows: "No human being in this world exists who does not love anything. Each person has his own place of love, different from others. Somebody loves his children, others love money and wealth. Many others love their physical body, house and prosperity, honour and awards, fame or pursuit of learning. In short, when the entire love of pleasures of senses gathers together and melts in the mould of God's form, it emerges as *Bhakti*." (Translated from original Marathi *Shri Sai Satcharitra*, Chapter 10, verses 126-128.)

Types of Bhakti

There are two aspects of God or *Brahman* — *Nirguna* (Unmanifested) and *Saguna* (Manifested). The *Nirguna* is formless while the *Saguna* is with form, though both denote the same *Brahman*. Some prefer the former and some the latter. As stated in the *Gita* (Chapter 12) the worship of the latter is easy and preferable. As man has got a form (body, senses, etc), it is natural and easy for him to worship God with form. Our love and devotion do not develop unless we worship *Saguna Brahman* for a certain period of time, and as we advance, it leads us to the worship (meditation) of *Nirguna Brahman*.

Sai Baba, therefore, not only professed *Saguna Bhakti* to his devotees but also tried to convince them about its effectiveness by giving them personal experiences. In fact, Sai Baba perhaps is the only saint who has given such experiences for the spread of *Saguna Bhakti*.

A devout person named Balabuva from Bombay, on account of his piety and worship, was known as 'Modern Tukaram'. He came to Shirdi for the first time in 1917. When he bowed before Baba, the latter said, "I know this man since four years." Balabuva wondered and thought. 'How could this be, as this is my first trip to Shirdi?' But thinking about it seriously he recollected that he had prostrated four years ago before Baba's portrait at Bombay and was convinced about the significance of Baba's words. He thought, 'How omniscient and all-pervarding are the saints and how kind they are to their *bhaktas*! I merely bowed to his photo: this fact was noticed by Baba and in due time he made me realise that seeing his photo is equivalent to seeing him in person." (Chapter 33)

In Chapter 9, we can read of the experience of Babasaheb Tarkhad of Bandra and his wife and son. Babasaheb Tarkhad was a member of Prarthana Samaj and did not believe in the worship of idols and pictures of God or *Sadguru*. Once Babasaheb's wife and son went to Shirdi. In their absence the daily worship of Shri Sai Baba's portrait in the house and offering of sugar-candy as *naivedya* had to be performed by Babasaheb, who had stayed back. Although Babasaheb tried to perform the pooja rites sincerely like his son, one day in a hurry to go to work he forgot to offer the sugar-candy as *naivedya*. Immediately on the very day at Shirdi when Baba Saheb's wife and son went for Baba's *darshan*, Baba said to Mrs Tarkhad, "Mother ! I had been to your house at

Bandra with a view to having something to eat. I found the door locked. I somehow got inside and found to my regret that Mr Tarkhad had left nothing for me to eat. So I have returned unappeased." When later Babasaheb learnt about this statement of Baba, he was convinced that food and drink offered to the picture/idol of a God/saint reached them. Only devotion and faith to that effect was required.

In 1917, on the full moon day of Holi festival, Sai Baba appeared in Hemadpant's dream and told him that he would come to his house for meals on that day. Afterwards in the afternoon when all the guests had sat down for lunch and were about to start eating, two Muslim friends of Hemadpant, named Ali Mohammed and Ismu Mujavar, brought in a framed earthen picture of Sai Baba, as if to confirm Baba's words in Hemadpant's dream that morning (Chapter 40). Later during a chance meeting (Chapter 41), Ali Mohammed explained to Hemadpant how and why he had brought that picture to him on that day. Ali Mohammed had bought this picture of Sai Baba from a hawker and hung it on a wall in his house at Bandra along with pictures of other saints. After some days, while Ali Mohammed was staying with his brother-in-law at Bombay due to abscess on his leg, his house at Bandra was locked. His brother-in-law told him that to keep and worship pictures of saints in the house was idol-worship and against the tenets of Islam, and if he desired an early cure of his illness he should immediately remove them from his house. Accordingly, Ali Mohammed asked his clerk to collect all such pictures from his household at Bandra and hand them over to his brother-in-law for immersing them into the sea.

But surprisingly after three months, when Ali Mohammed got well and returned to his house at Bandra, he found Sai Baba's picture still hanging on the wall. He was at his wit's end and wanted to understand how Sai Baba's picture alone was not removed by his clerk with other pictures. Knowing Hemadpant to be a Sai devotee, he brought it and gave it to him on that day for safe custody. With this incident, Sai Baba not only convinced his devotees that he was present in his pictures also, but at the same time explained to a Muslim how idol-worship of Hindus was not incorrect or ill-placed.

When Kakasaheb Dixit invited Sai Baba to attend his son's thread ceremony at Nagpur and Nanasaheb Chandarkar his son's wedding at Gwalior, Baba asked them to take Shama alias Madhavrao Deshpande on his behalf. When Kakasaheb pressed him to himself attend, he added that he would also reach ahead of Shama after visiting Kashi (Benaras) and Prayag (Allahabad). When Shama reached Gaya, he found Baba present there in the priest's residence ahead of him in the form of a picture (Chapter 46).

In addition to giving such experiences to his devotees, Sai Baba also propagated worship of *Saguna* (Manifested) form through his actions and advice. At Shirdi, he not only carried out repairs of old temples through his rich devotees but refused to allow any of his devotees to perform his Puja unless all the idols in all the temples in Shirdi were first worshipped. We also know how he used to present silver coins to his devotees to be kept in their puja-rooms for worshipping and encourage some devotees like Mrs M. W. Pradhan to worship his silver *padukas* (*sandals*).

Nine Forms of Bhakti

There are nine forms of *Saguna Bhakti* mentioned in Chapter 21: (1) *Shravan* (hearing the praises), (2) *Kirtan* (singing the praises), (3) *Smarana* (remembering the form and the name),

(4) *Pada sevana* (service of the feet), (5) *Archana* (worship), (6) *Vandana* (bowing), (7) *Dasya* (service), (8) *Sakhya* (friendship), and (9) *Atma-nivedan* (surrendering). "If any one of these is faithfully followed, Lord Hari (Krishna) will be pleased and manifest Himself in the heart of the devotee," adds Dada Kelkar in the same chapter. Sai Baba, time and again, used to refer to these nine forms directly or indirectly throughout his talks and actions, eg, parable of nine balls of stool in Chapter 21, returning consecrated nine rupees in ash to Appasaheb Kulkarni, in Chapter 23, and giving nine rupees to Laxmibai Shinde just before passing away, in Chapter 41. In addition, Sai Baba got these forms properly executed by His devotees.

1) *Shravan (Hearing the Praises)*

Sai Baba used to ask educated devotees like Kakasaheb Dixit and Bapusaheb Jog to read out the *Jnaneshwari, Eknathi Bhagawat* and *Bhavarth Ramayana* to others regularly and send other devotees to hear them. About *Shri Sai Satcharita* also Sai Baba himself has said: "Hearing My stories and teachings will create faith in the devotees' hearts and they will easily get self-realisation and bliss." (Chapter 2, p. 6)

2) *Kirtan (Singing the Praises)*

We also know how Sai Baba, on occasions like Rama-Navami (birth-anniversary of Shri Rama), and Gokulashtami (birth anniversary of Shri Krishna) used to get *kirtans* (singing the praises of God with music) performed by *kirtankars,* in the open space in front of Dwarkamai. We see, in Chapter 15, Sai Baba insisting Das Ganu to dress during *kirtans* like Sage Narada without any paraphernalia — bare from waist upwards with only a garland round the neck and a pair of *chiplis* in one hand. Actually it was Sai Baba who made Das Ganu give up his service in the Police department and take to singing God's praises.

In Chapter 3, Sai Baba says: "If a man earnestly sings about My life and My deeds, him I shall beset in front and back and on all sides. Believe Me that if anybody sings My *leelas*, I will give him infinite joy and ever-lasting contentment." (Chapter 2, p. 10)

Look at Chapter 3 again. How loudly and in harsh tones Rohilla was reciting *Kalamas* (verses from the *Holy Quran*) and shouting "Allah ho Akbar" (God is Great)! The villagers who could not get sleep properly due to this nuisance complained to Baba but Baba liked the prayers and cries to God better than anything else and so he encouraged Rohilla and asked the villagers to wait and suffer the nuisance quietly.

3) *Smarana (Remembering the Form and the Name)*

Smarana means *nama-smarana*, ie, constantly repeating the name of God by remembering His form. *Shri Sai Satcharita* says: "The effectiveness of God's name is well known. It saves us from all sins and bad tendencies, frees us from the cycles of births and deaths. There is no easier *sadhana* than this. It is the best purifier of our mind. It requires no paraphernalia and no restrictions." (Chapter 27, p. 145)

No wonder therefore that in Chapter 27 we see that Sai Baba forced his intimate devotee Shama to accept Ramdasi's copy of *Vishnu Sahasranama* (a booklet containing thousand names of Shri Vishnu) and learn to recite it.

Similarly, about the efficacy of his own name Sai Baba himself says: "If a man utters My name with love, I shall fulfil all his wishes, and increase his devotion." (Chapter 3,

p. 10) "If you always say 'Sai Sai', I shall take you over the seven seas. Believe in these words and you will be certainly benefited." (Chapter 13, p. 73)

4) *Padasevan (Service of the Feet)*

Padasevan means salutation to the deity of worship or Guru by respectfully touching his feet with both hands and resting one's head on them or massaging them. *Padasevan* also includes remembering and meditating on feet.

In this connection read in *Shri Sai Satcharita* the following description of Sai Baba's usual pose of sitting on a stone with his right leg held across the left knee: "The fingers of his left hand are spread on the right foot. On the right toe are spread his two fingers — index and middle ones. By this picture Baba means to say, as it were, 'If you want to see my Light, be egoless and most humble and meditate on my right toe through two openings between the two — index and middle fingers — and you will see my Light. This is the easiest means of attaining devotion." (Chapter 22, p. 116)

Also look at Sai Baba's oil painting in Dwarkamai. Therein, Baba is sitting with the right foot forward. Similarly, in the picture along with Mhalsapati and Shama, Baba is sitting with both legs spread out in front, as if making it convenient for devotees to salute or massage them. In short, Baba encouraged the method of *Padasevan Bhakti*.

To drink the water used for washing the feet of one's deity or *sadguru* or to sprinkle it on one's head as a symbol of bath is also part of *Padasevan*. As seen in Chapter 4, Sai Baba convinced Das Ganu that such water is as holy and meritorious as the waters of the Ganga and the Yamuna rivers at their confluence at Prayag (Allahabad) which he proved by miraculously making the streams of water of these rivers flow through both his toes. Similarly in Chapter 45, we see when Kakasaheb Dixit had doubts about his own *bhakti* after reading in Chapter 2 of *Eknath Bhagwat* about the very tough *bhakti* of nine *Natha's* or *Siddhas* of Rishabha dynasty, how Sai Baba arranged the narration of Anandrao Pakhade's dream for convincing Kakasaheb that bowing to the feet of one's deity or guru is a quite sufficient form of *bhakti*.

5) Archana (Worship)

Archana means worship of one's deity or guru in person or through his picture or idol. This includes bathing feet, applying sandalpaste on the forehead, decorating with clothes and flowers, waving of lights and offering *naivedya*, etc. In the beginning, Sai Baba did not allow his devotees to perform any such worship. But later on, due to the insistence of devotees, he allowed them to do so, and even today Sai Baba's worship is being carried on in the same manner daily in the Samadhi Mandir at Shirdi. Similarly, worship of *Sadguru* on *Guru Poornima* also was started by Sai Baba due to the insistence of Dada Kelkar, Tatyasaheb Noolkar and Madhavrao Deshpande.

6) Vandana (Bowing)

Sai Baba never bothered about whether a person visiting him bowed to him or not. However sometimes Baba did make Mulay Shastri, an orthodox Agnihotri Brahmin of Nasik (Chapter 12), or a doctor devotee of Rama or (Chapter 35) Kaka Mahajani's master Sheth Thakkar Dharamsey, bow down to him by showing some miracles. But this was only to convince them and other devotees present the importance of bowing down and surrendering respectfully before a saint and not for showing his own importance or greatness. Bowing down helps to shed one's conceit and vanity and to increase humility and humbleness. Hemadpant describes his experience when he first bowed down to Sai Baba at Shirdi: "I ran and prostated before Baba and then my joy knew no bounds. All my senses were satisfied and I forgot thirst and hunger. The moment I touched Sai Baba's feet, I began a new lease of life." (Chapter2, p. 7)

7) *Dasya (Service)*

Examples of this method in *Shri Sai Satcharita* are Abdul of Nanded, Balaji Patil of Nevasa and Radhakrishna Mai of Pandharpur. Abdul came to Baba at the young age of 19 years, leaving his wife and children, and served Baba continuously for 26 long years until Baba's Mahasamadhi. His main job was to keep the lamps at Dwarkamai, *chavadi* and Lendi Baug burning by pouring oil into them. He also used to daily sweep the masjid, fill up drinking water in the earthen waterpot, and wash Baba's clothes in Lendi Nullah. After Baba's attaining *Samadhi* he did not leave Shirdi to go back to his wife and children but continued to sweep and maintain Baba's Samadhi and guide devotees visiting Shirdi.

Balaji Patil of Nevasa used to drink only that water which came out of the channel where Baba used to bathe and wash his hands and feet. On Baba's instructions, he used to perform even the dirtiest and difficult services of tending to the sick in Shirdi. He was the first devotee who thought of sweeping the tracks used by Baba for going to Lendi Baug and *chavadi*. Every year he used to bring all the grains produced in his field to Shirdi, place them before Baba and carry back only what Baba returned to him. No wonder therefore that when Damuanna of Ahmednagar once

requested Baba to come for meals, Baba asked him to take
Balaji Patil as his representative and warned Damuanna to
treat him as an honoured guest. Similarly, at the time of the
death anniversary of Balaji, when the guests arrived threefold
in numbers, Baba made sure that the food remained sufficient
till the end and saved the prestige of Balaji's family.

Radhakrishna Mai was a beautiful young widow in her
thirties. She never came to the masjid during Baba's presence
and always covered her face with the end of her saree in
front of Baba. However, she diligently and regularly carried
out the task of renovating the masjid with cowdung paste
from time to time, decorating the sleeping room in the
chavadi with mirrors, pictures, chandeliers, etc, and
procuring from rich devotees dresses, ornaments, umbrellas,
lamps, etc, for the *chavadi* procession of Baba. Even though
of the brahmin caste, she did not hesitate after Balaji Patil's
death to perform his task of sweeping and removing excreta
and dung from tracks that Baba used for going to Lendi
Baug and *chavadi*. No wonder therefore that Baba daily sent
bread with cooked vegetables at noon time out of love and
affection for her and even sent his elderly and educated
devotees like Babasaheb Rege of Indore, Bapusaheb Butty
of Nagpur, Kakasaheb Dixit of Bombay and Wamanrao
Patel (Swamy Sharananjadaji) also of Bombay to learn
lessons of *bhakti* from her.

8) *Sakhya (Friendship)*

In *Shri Sai Satcharita* the only unique example of *Sakhya
Bhakti* is that of Shama alias Madhavrao Deshpande. He
had spent about 42 to 43 years continuously in Baba's
company, except perhaps for Tatya Kote Patil and
Mhalsapati nobody else had this great fortune. But

Madhavrao's close friendship with Baba was unique. Baba used to address him out of love and fondness as 'Shama' and Madhavrao in return used to address Baba as 'Deva', ie, God. Madhavrao had also the unique privilege of addressing Baba singularly on familiar terms. No one else could dare to talk to Baba in such a manner nor could anyone argue with him so boldly.

In Chapter 36, we see how Baba once jokingly had even pinched Shama on the cheek, and in the same chapter we see how Madhavrao had said to Mrs Aurangabadkar who had presented a coconut to Baba with the hope of getting a son : "Dear madam ! You are the witness to my words. If within 12 months you do not get any issue, I will break a coconut against this Deva's head and drive Him out of this Masjid." (p. 203).

What audacity ! Who else could speak such words to Baba who was known to get into sudden fits of anger and even hit the devotees with his stick (*sataka*)!

At the same time, Madhavrao's *bhakti* was also great. Once Madhavrao was sleeping in Dixit Wada and Kakasaheb Dixit went to wake him up. Just then Kakasaheb heard words 'Shri Sainath Maharaj', 'Shri Sainath Maharaj' coming out from Madhavrao's body in a torrent. No wonder then that Baba went out of his way to see that Madhavrao was comfortable and happy in his life. In Chapter 46, we see how Baba arranged for Madhavrao's comfortable pilgrimage to Kashi, Gaya and Prayag free of cost. After Baba's *nirvana* Madhavrao lived for 22 years and Baba made sure that his most pet devotee was looked after with prestige and comfort. Many millionaires and rulers of States used to bow down to Madhavrao and lovingly embrace him, taking him with them on pilgrimages in comfort. Indeed *Sakhya Bhakti* or devotion by friendship is great. Did not Lord Krishna Himself drive Arjuna's chariot during the Mahabharata war!

9) *Atma-nivedan (Surrender)*

Atma-nivedan means complete surrender to God. In this form or type, the devotee not only surrenders his wife and children and his entire movable and immovable property but also his intellect and egoism, ie, assertion of personal doing also, to his deity of worship or guru. This form of *bhakti* is so important that Saint Ramdas states that without *Atma-nivedan* or complete surrender of self, there is no escape from the chain of births and deaths. *Smarana* is the beginning and *Atma-nivedan* is the end of *bhakti*.

Of *Atma-nivedan*, the best example in *Shri Sai Satcharita* is that of Kakasaheb Dixit. He used to stay at Shirdi frequently for many days continuously leaving his prosperous legal practice, high social status and even his wife and children at Bombay. Once when I was in London, while boarding a train, he fell down and became lame for life. Yet he never requested Baba to cure his leg but only, "To bring round his lame fickle mind and to give him eternal bliss" (Chapter 50, p. 266). Kakasaheb's surrender to Baba was complete — both mentally and physically. Once Kakasaheb earned a lot of money in a Maharaja's case as a fee. He put all the silver coins in a big trunk, brought it to Shirdi and placing it in front of Baba, said, "Baba ! All this is yours." Baba said, "Is that so?" and opening the trunk, he distributed with both hands all the coins to the devotees present to his heart's content, and in a few minutes the trunk was empty. At that time Shri Garde, the Sub-Judge of Nagpur, and another friend of Kakasaheb, were present. They were watching Kakasaheb's face intently. But surprisingly, they did not find Kakasaheb's face even slightly disturbed at the sight of his hard earnings being dispensed of so quickly and recklessly. What a great renunciation and what a complete surrender to the sadguru! (Chapter 45, p. 251)

Once Baba asked Kakasaheb to kill a goat with a knife, and although a brahmin by caste and had, never known killing in his lifetime, Kakasaheb immediately got ready to do so. He said to Baba : "Your nectar-like word is law unto us, we do not know any other ordinance. We remember you always, meditate on your form and obey you day and night. We do not know or consider whether it is right or wrong to kill. We do not want to reason or discuss things, but implicit and prompt compliance with Guru's orders is our duty and *dharma.*" (Chapter 23, p. 126)

During Baba's lifetime, Kakasaheb never did any important thing without consulting Baba, and the same practice he carried on after Baba's attaining *samadhi* by placing chits in front of Baba's picture and getting one picked up by a small child, considering it as Baba's answer. He used to say, "When the body is surrendered completely to Guru, what right have we on its functioning?"

No wonder therefore that Hemadpant in his Marathi *Shri Sai Satcharita* has described Kakasaheb as 'बावनकसी सुवर्ण' — Gold purified fifty-two times, in other words, very pure and excellent gold (Chapter 23, Verse 135). Baba also promised him that "He would take him in a balloon, ie, secure him a happy death" (Chapter 50, p. 267), and he actually did so. On July 5, 1926, Kakasaheb, in the company of Annasaheb Dabholkar, was travelling in the local train at Bombay and while talking about Baba, all of a sudden threw his neck on Dabholkar's shoulders and breathed his last with no trace of pain or uneasiness. It was *Ekadashi,* ie, the eleventh day of the Hindu calendar, considered very holy, especially for death.

Sai Baba's Most Simple but Effective Method

Thus we have seen the nine forms of *bhakti* as mentioned in our scriptures and how Sai Baba got them properly executed by his devotees. However, Baba told Radhabai Deshmukh, who was insisting on getting a *mantra* or *updesh* from him, a very simple but most effective form of Bhakti: "Look at Me wholeheartedly and I in turn will look at you similarly."

Actually this is another form of *Smarana Bhakti*, ie, meditation. Later Baba said to Hemadpant: "Meditate always on my formless nature which is knowledge incarnate, consciousness and bliss. If you cannot do this, meditate on My form, top to toe as you see here night and day. As you go on doing this, your *vritties* will be one-pointed and the distinction between the *Dhyata* (meditator), *Dhyana* (meditation) and *Dheya* (thing meditated on) will be lost and the meditator will be one with the consciousness and be merged in the Brahma."

"The mother tortoise is on one bank of the river and her young ones are on the other side. She gives neither milk, nor warmth to them. Her mere glance gives them nutrition. The young ones do nothing but remember (meditate upon) their mother. The tortoise's glance is to the young ones a downpour of nectar, the only source of sustenance and happiness. Similar is the relation between the Guru and disciples."

— *Chapter 19, pp. 99-100*

Actually whether you meditate on any form with love or hatred, the result is the same — you are transformed into that form. See the examples of Ravana, Kansa and the insect caught in the spider's net.

What is Ideal Bhakti?

First and foremost, *bhakti* should be out of great love for the deity of worship or guru and full faith in his greatness or superiority. It is not important how costly or rich your offering is or how many hours you worship him. It is sincerity of that offering which is important. In Chapter 16, we see Hemadpant saying about Baba, "He would accept with appreciation any small thing offered with love and devotion but if the same thing was offered with pride and haughtiness, He would reject it."

— *Chapter 16, p. 87*

Baba says: "I do not need any paraphernalia of worship either eight fold or sixteen fold. I rest where there is full devotion." (Chapter 13, p. 73)

And Lord Krishna has said the same thing in the *Gita*:

पत्रं पुष्पं फलं तोयं यो मे भकत्या प्रयच्छति।
तदहं भकत्यु पहतमश्रामि प्रयतात्मनः ।।अ. 26।।

(Whoever offers to me with love a leaf, a flower, a fruit or even water, I appear in person before that disinterested devotee or purified intellect, and delightfully partake of that article offered by him with love.)

— *Chapter 9, Verse 26*

Secondly, *bhakti* should be without any expectation. Worshipping a deity or *sadguru* to gain something and making a vow for such fulfillment becomes business. If something has to be demanded from God, what should it be? *Shri Sai Satcharita* has some noble examples. For instance, when Baba pinched Shama on his cheek, see what he said to Baba: "We do not want any respect from you or heaven, balloon, etc. Let our faith unto your feet be ever wide awake." (Chapter 36, p. 203) While describing how Amir

Shakkar was reminded of God or Allah, ie, Sai Baba, when he suffered from rheumatism, Hemadpant in his Marathi *Shri Sai Satcharita* quotes the example of Kunti, the mother of the Pandavas. When the Mahabharata war was over and Lord Krishna asked Kunti her wishes, although tired of living in concealment and forests and fatigued with innumerable calamities, Kunti said, "Krishna, happiness to those others who are asking for it but to me give only calamities again and again, since that will make me remember His name again and again without break."

— Chapter 22, Verses 110-112

Similarly, look at Hemadpant's demand to Sai Baba in his epilogue of *Shri Sai Satcharita*: "Let not our mind wander and desire anything except Thee. Let his work (*Satcharita*) be in every house and let it be studied daily. Ward off all the calamities of those who study it regularly." Thus a demand, if at all, should be for everlasting, wishing *bhakti* and for welfare of others.

Again for ideal *bhakti*, Sai Baba has given to the devotees a maxim of two words — *Shraddha* (Firm Faith) and *Saburi* (Patience). One should have firm faith in one's deity of worship or *Sadguru* that whatever he does for us is for our ultimate good. Patience means courage during calamities and not to let your devotion to your Sadguru weaken even slightly in spite of early reverses. Really these two qualities are bound to give an extra fine edge to one's *bhakti*.

Sai Baba has mentioned a very important point about *bhakti*. According to him, *bhakti* would be steady and one-pointed, like that of a chaste woman to her husband. He disapproved of anybody giving up the devotion of *Sadgurus* as per family traditions or previous associations and coming

to him for *upadesh*. See what he said to Mr Pant, a disciple
of another guru, who came to him for *darshan* : "Come
what may, leave not, but stick to your bolster (support or
guru) and always remain in union with him."
— *Chapter 26, p. 139*

Again in Chapter 14, Sai says: "There are innumerable
saints in this world, but our father (Guru) is the real father
(Real Guru). Others might say many good things, but we
should never forget our Guru's words." (p. 244)

Sai Baba revived Bhagvantrao Kshirsagar's original *bhakti*
of Vithal and *bhakti* of Akkalkot Swami in case of
Harishchandra Pitale and Gopal Ambedkar (Chapter 4). He
actually got angry with his devotee Nanasaheb Chandorkar
for avoiding the shrine of Dattatreya at Kopargaon in a hurry
to come to Shirdi (Chapter 26).

Sai Baba wanted to impress upon his devotees that all
deities of worship and *sadgurus* are one and the same and so
they need not go on changing them again and again. To
prove this, he used to give them visions in the form of Vithal,
Shri Rama, Dattatreya, Maruti (Hanuman) according to their
deities of worship and also show by miracles the identity
with their saints as with Gholap Swami (Chapter 12),
Kanarese saint (Appa) (Chapter 21) and Mouli Saheb
(Chapter 14).

In the original Marathi *Shri Sai Satcharita*, there are some
beautiful statements explaining by examples how to worship
Sai Baba : "One should tie one's mind firmly to *Sadguru's*
feet just as a calf who, though thoroughly satisfied by
drinking her mother's milk, does not move away from her."
— *Chapter 37, Verse 77*

"The image of Sai Baba should constantly be in our mind
during our day-to-day work just as in the case of a miser, in

whatever distant town or city he is roaming about, the treasure hidden at home is constantly in front of his eyes."

— *Chapter 3, Verse 185*

"An ant does not leave the piece of jaggery (due to its addiction to the sweetness) even if its head breaks away from its body. Similarly one should stick to the feet of one's deities of worship or *Sadguru*, firmly."

— *Chapter 27, Verse 171*

Sai Baba's Assurances

I shall end this article by listing some assurances given by Sai Baba to his devotees:

"My man (Devotee) be at any distance, a thousand *cos* away from Me, he will be drawn to Shirdi like a sparrow with a thread tied to its feet."

— *Chapter 27, p. 150*

"There will never be any dearth or scarcity regarding food and clothes in My devotees' homes."

— *Chapter 6, p. 31*

"Go wherever you will over the whole world, I am with you. My abode is in your heart and I am within you. Worship Me always, who is seated in your heart, as well as in the hearts of all beings. Blessed and fortunate indeed is he who knows Me thus."

— *Chapter 15, p. 86*

"Believe Me, though I pass away, My bones in my tomb will give you hope and confidence. Not only Myself but My tomb would be speaking, moving and communicating with those who would surrender themselves wholeheartedly to Me. Do not be anxious that I would be absent from you.

You will hear My bones speaking and discussing your welfare. But remember Me, always, believe in Me, heart and soul and then you will be most benefited."

— *Chapter 25, p. 136*

5

CYCLES OF REBIRTH

Although Sai Baba lived in a masjid and dressed like a Muslim *fakir*, he believed in the Hindu theory of rebirth. During his talks to Hindu devotees, he not only referred time and again to this theory, but by performing some miracles tried to convince them of this theory.

One day after lunch, when Shama, the pet devotee of Sai Baba, was drying his wet hands with a towel, Baba pinched Shama's cheek. Shama feigning anger, said, "Deva! Is it proper for you to pinch me like this? We don't want such a mischievous God who pinches us thus. Are we your dependents? Is this the fruit of your intimacy?"

Thereupon Baba said: "Oh Shama, during the 72 generations that you were with Me, I never touched you till now and now you resent My pinching you just once out of fun!" (Chapter 36, pp. 202, 203)

Similarly, to Durandhar brothers he said, "We are acquainted with each other for the last 60 generations." (Chapter 51, p. 269)

"Sai Baba's another devotee, Shri Nanasaheb Chandorkar, was then Secretary to the Collector at Ahmednagar. Sai Baba sent a message to him not once but three times with Appa Kulkarni, the village accountant, to come to him. At last Chandorkar came to Shirdi and asked Baba why he had called him. Thereupon Baba said, "In the whole world, is there only one Nana? Then shouldn't there be some reason when I called only you? Myself and you have been together during the last four births. You are not aware of this but I know it."

In Chapter 4 of the *Gita*, Lord Krishna said the same thing to Arjuna :

बहूनि मे व्यतीतानि, जन्मानि तवचार्जुन ।
तान्यहं वेद सर्वाणि, न त्वं वेत्थ परंतप ।।5।।

(Arjuna! You and I have passed through many births, I know them well, while you do not, O, Scorcher of foes!)

Some *dervishes* (strolling mendicants among Mohammedans maintaining themselves by exhibiting antics of bears, monkeys, etc) brought before Baba a tiger suffering some agony. On approaching Baba the tiger breathed his last and the *dervishes* were filled with dejection and sorrow at the loss of their only means of maintenance. While consoling them, we find Baba referring to the theory of rebirth: "The tiger was your debtor from previous birth. He paid off the debts by serving you in this life and when his debt was paid off, he was free and met the death at My feet." (Chapter 31)

One noon, Dadasaheb Khaparde's wife brought a dish containing *sanza* (wheat pudding), *purees*, rice, soup and *kheer* (sweet rice) and other sundry articles to the masjid. Baba, who usually waited for hours, got up at once, went up to his dining seat and removing, the outer covering from the dish, began to partake of the things hungrily. Shama then asked him, "Why this partiality? You throw away dishes of others and do not care to look at them, but this dish you draw to earnestly and do justice to it thoroughly. Is the dish of this woman so sweet?"

Baba then replied: "This food is really extraordinary. In former birth, this lady was a merchant's fat cow yielding much milk. Then she disappeared and took birth in a gardener's family, then in a *kshatriya* family and married a merchant. Then she was born in a Brahmin's family. I saw her after a very long time, let me take some sweet morsels of love from her dish." (Chapter 27, p. 148)

Thus, by narrating the lady's tale of many previous births, Baba probably explained to his devotees how a soul can progressively rise from an animal form to a human form and then to a Brahmin birth on account of virtuous deeds.

Sai Baba was omniscient, ie, before him the past, present and future were open to view. Hence once, by giving the details of previous births and foretelling the places of future births of a boy called 'Babu', he convinced everybody that a soul is born again and again.

This story is narrated in H. H. Narasimha Swamiji's devotees, experiences of Sri Sai Baba (p. 114), in the statement of Rao Bahadur H. V. Sathe : "Baba was greatly attracted to Dada Kelkar's (ie, my father-in-law's) nephew Babu. He was a measurer under my assistant Limaye (I was then Asst Supdt of Revenue Survey of Kopargaon and Yeola). But instead of paying due attention to his official work, he would go and stay at Shirdi doing service to Baba. My assistant complained to me that my brother-in-law (Babu) was always going away to Shirdi and neglecting his work. I communicated this to Kelkar and he said, 'What is to be done? He is guided and ordered by Baba.' In fact, Baba, knowing evidently what was to happen to Babu shortly, made light of his service and said, 'Blast the service. Let him serve me.' Babu was always attending on Baba and rendering as much service as he could and Baba would always see that Babu got the choicest delicacies when they were available. So Limaye also let him do as he liked. In a few days Babu passed away, aged only 22 leaving an issueless widow."

In the same connection see what Moreshwar W. Pradhan of Santacruz has to say in his statement (pp. 96-98) : "On the day we reached Shirdi, Baba said, to Madhavrao Deshpande pointing to my wife, 'This is the mother of my Babu.' Mr Chandorkar thought it must refer obviously to my sister-in-law who was believed to be pregnant and asked Baba, pointing to my sister-in-law, 'This is the lady, is it not?' Baba replied, 'No, It is this,' and he again pointed to my wife."

"Exactly twelve months from that date, my wife delivered a male child and we have named that son 'Babu' (the name used by Baba).

"When Babu was four months old, we carried him to Shirdi. Sai Baba took Babu up in his arms and endearingly addressed Babu thus : 'Babu ! Where had you been ? Were you vexed with or weary of Me?' To mark the joyous arrival of Babu at Shirdi, Baba pulled out two rupees from his pocket, got *burfi* (sweets) for the amount and distributed exactly as they do on the occasion of a son's birth. On this occasion Baba also said, 'Babu's bungalow is beautiful and ready.' Surely, Baba's words were soon fulfilled by my purchase of the bungalow I was living in."

On reading the above two statements, I am sure that readers will not only be convinced regarding the theory of rebirths but also will realise how Baba cared to look after his devotees from birth to birth.

While talking about rebirths, Sai Baba always said that these births, whether happy or full of miseries, one gets according to one's previous deeds only. For instance, see how, in Chapters 46 and 47, after narrating the past and present lives of two goats and the frog and the snake, Sai Baba concludes : "The moral of the story is that one has to reap what one sows and there is no escape unless one suffers and squares up one's old debts and dealings with others." (p. 254)

That is why Sai Baba advised his devotees to always act honestly and with integrity, keeping one's conscience awake to what is right and what is wrong. He always used to say, "जैसी जिसकी नियत, वैसी उसकू बर्कत" (If you act in a good way, good really will follow). (p. 75)

In Chapter 14 again, Dabholkar quotes the *Brihadaranyaka Upanishad* which says that Lord Prajapti advised the gods, men and demons by one letter — 'Da'. The gods understood by this letter that they should practise (1) *Dama*, ie, self-control, the men should practise (2) *Dana*, ie, charity; the demons understood that they should practise (3) *Daya*, ie, compassion. Thus to men charity or giving was recommended. In order to teach the devotees the lesson of charity and to remove their attachments to money and thus purify their minds, Baba extracted *dakshina* from them.

Again he used to stress, "We get human body as a result of merits in past births and it is worthwhile that with its aid we should attain devotion and liberation in this life. So we should never be lazy but always be on the alert to gain our end and aim of life." (p. 78)

In Chapter 8 also, Sai Baba has said the same thing, "Four things are common to all the creatures, viz, food, sleep, fear and sexual union. In the case of man, he is endowed with a special faculty, viz, knowledge, with the help of which he can attain God-vision, which is impossible in other births." (p. 45)

It is said that the last wish or thought a man has at the hour of death determines his future course. Lord Krishna has also said in the *Gita* (Chapter 8 *Slokas* 5 and

6) that "he who remembers Me in his last moments comes verily to Me, and he that meditates otherwise at the time goes to what he looks for."

We cannot be certain that we can entertain particular good thoughts at our moment of death for various reasons, viz, pain caused by diseases, worries about our families, future, etc. All saints therefore recommend us to practise remembering God and chanting His name constantly so that we may not get puzzled when the time for departure comes. Wise devotees practise a still simpler device to achieve this goal. They approach the saints in their last moments, surrender completely to them trusting that the all-knowing saints would do the needful. In *Shri Sai Satcharita* (Chapter 31), five such examples are quoted, viz, Vijayanand Sanyasi, Balaram Mankar, Tatyasaheb Noolkar, Megha and the tiger of *dervishes*. All of them breathed their last in the presence of Baba at Shirdi.

Thus, Sai Baba not only talked about the theory of rebirths of his devotees, but also explained to them how to ensure a good rebirth or complete escape from births.

6

THEORY OF 'KARMA'

Although it is usually said that the theory of *karma* is difficult to comprehend, if one recalls the scientific principle of 'Action and reaction', it would be understood easily. In everyday life, whatever we do, we have to bear the results, sometimes immediately, sometimes later. For instance, if we touch fire, our hand will be burnt immediately and if we smoke cigarettes or take heavy alcoholic liquors, after sometime our body becomes a prey to various diseases. On the same principle, whatever consequences of our good or bad actions performed in our past lives have remained to be experienced, one has to experience them in this life. There is no way out of it.

"The moral of the story is that one has to reap what one sows and there is no escape unless one suffers and squares up one's old debts and dealings with others."

— *Chapter 47, p. 254*

"Jaise Jiski Niyat, Vaise Uski Barkat"
(If you act in a good way, good really will follow)
- Sai Baba to Raghuvir Purandare

Always Do Good Deeds

Sai Baba, therefore, preached to his devotees to act according to the teachings of scriptures only : "Everyone should behave honestly (virtuously) and keep his conscience awake (to decide what is right and what is wrong). We should do our duty sincerely but without accepting the pride of doership, which should be dedicated along with its fruits or results to God, so that we will remain aloof without the actions binding us.

"We should act lovingly towards all the beings. We should not indulge in arguments. If anybody rebukes us, we should learn to bear the same calmly. Words of rebuke do not cause holes in our body. We should not rival with others nor slander others. What others do, we should not bother about. Their actions with them and ours with us.

"Always be working. Do not sit idle. Remember God's name. Read religious books."

— Sai Baba's teachings, in a nutshell, as given by Kakasaheb Dixit in his preface to Smt Savitribai Tendulkar's book *Sainath Bhajan Mala.*

In our scriptures (*Taittiriya Upanishad*) the importance of charity is greatly stressed : "Charity should be with faith. Charity without faith is useless. Give with magnamity, ie, liberally, give with modesty, with awe and sympathy."

— *Chapter 14, p. 81*

Sai Baba also stressed the same : "Shri Hari (God) will be certainly pleased if you give water to the thirsty, bread to the hungry, clothes to the naked and your verandah to the needy for sitting and resting."

— *Chapter 14, p. 81*

However, while performing good deeds, Baba has given a special warning not to do a particular deed because others do it. One must think of one's physical, financial and even spiritual capacity. This has been illustrated in Chapter 45, where Baba rejected the offer of Kakasaheb Dixit for providing another wooden plank for hanging high on the ceiling for Mhalsapati, similar to Baba's.

Similarly, about running around and trying advices of various Gurus, see what Baba says : "There are innumerable saints in the world, but our father (Guru) is the real father (Real Guru). Others might say many good things, but we should never forget our Guru's advice, because he knows what is best for us."

— *Chapter 45, p. 244*

Seek Company of Saints

As regards atheists, irreligious and wicked persons, Sai Baba advised his devotees to shun their company altogether. Instead, he used to ask his devotees to seek the company of saints : "The importance of the company of the saints is very great. If you take refuge in them (saints) wholeheartedly, they will carry you off safely across the ocean of worldly existence. It is for this reason that the saints manifest themselves in this world. Even sacred rivers such as the Ganga and the Godavari, etc, which wash away the sins of the world, declare that saints should come to them for bath and purify them."

— *Chapter 10, p. 62*

Even hearing the stories of the saints or reading the books, written by them, is in a way, keeping their company.

Avoid Bad Deeds

Sai Baba used to say repeatedly that debt, enmity and murder follow a person till the end of the world. In other words, one can never escape to suffer their consequences.

Debt may be of any kind, eg, money, food, or even service. One has to repay it, if not in this life, at least in the next. In Chapter 31, we see that when the sick tiger, who was brought before Sai Baba for cure, died in front of him, the *dervishes* were dejected at the loss of their means of subsistence. On that occasion see what Baba said to them: The tiger was your debtor in previous life. He was born again and stayed under your bondage until his debt was repaid."

— Chapter 31, Verse 163

That is why when somebody asked Baba why he paid Rs. 2 to the person who merely brought a ladder and placed it against a wall, Baba replied: "Nobody should take the labour of others in vain. The worker should be paid his dues promptly and liberally."

— Chapter 19, p. 105

In short, money, food or even small service from others should be promptly repaid, if not in cash at least in kind. We have heard how Baba himself used to repair the walls of the masjid or spread cowdung on its floor, without accepting anybody's help. Similarly, whenever Baba desired to perform the charity of feeding poor persons, he made all the preparations from beginning to end by himself, like buying corn, flour, spices from the market, grinding, cooking and distributing also.

In this context, Sai Baba especially urged his devotees to avoid greed for money since it leads to enmity and sometimes even to murder. We know how this has been so effectively stressed by Baba by narrating the stories of the past lives of two goats in Chapter 46 and of the frog and the serpent in Chapter 47.

"The moral of the story is that greed for money drags man to the lowest level and ultimately brings destruction on him and others."

— Chapter 45, p. 254

Sai Baba's demanding *dakshina* from devotees was also aimed at removing their attachment to money. He did not keep the collection with himself but distributed it amongst the devotees and the poor by the end of the day — an example of renunciation himself.

Obstacles in Carrying out Good Deeds

Many a time even if a person tries to do good deeds and behave as per the scriptures, he is unable to do so and is led on to the evil path. Why should this happen? This is because of his deeds in the past life and his nature formed accordingly.

Also there is another obstruction when one is deciding to perform a good deed. Someone of an evil nature advises you not to proceed with a particular act. Hence, if you try hard to get over his bad nature and not listen to the evil advice, you will certainly reach the goal.

Sai Baba always helped his devotees with their good determinations. For instance, he encouraged the good determination of Dabholkar to sing unceasingly Rama's name during one Thursday, by arranging the coincidence of making Dabholkar listen to a song sung by one Aurangabadkar on Rama (Chapter 19).

However, Baba regretted that very few of his devotees came to him for spiritual gain. They only came for wealth, health, power, honour, position, cure of diseases and other temporal gains: "My Sircar's treasury (spiritual wealth) is full. It is overflowing. I say, dig out and take away this wealth in cartloads. The blessed son of a true mother should fill himself with this wealth. This opportunity wont't come again."

— *Chapter 32, p. 178*

Freedom from rebirths

Sometimes, it is argued that if we perform no acts at all, whether good or bad, there would be no good or bad consequences to suffer. Thus there will be an end to the chain of rebirths. Yes, but is it ever possible to live without doing anything? As long as one live, one has to do something. Even a *sanyasi* who has abandoned all worldly possessions and earthly affections, has to beg for food to quench his hunger. Even if he does live on whatever food is brought to him by others, he has to perform the act of chewing it and gulping it and bear the consequences of doing it correctly or incorrectly. Not only this, but since he has acquired the debt of receiving the food from others, he has to repay it in some form or another, whether in this life or the other.

Therefore, the only way to get freedom from rebirths is to perform whatever acts one has been destined to perform in this life or whatever good deeds one plans to perform, one should perform them with sincerity and integrity. But at the same time, one should not accept its doership with oneself and also its consequences, whether good or bad. Lord Krishna also advises the same thing in the *Gita* :

कर्मण्येवाधिकारस्ते मा फलेषु कदाचन।
मा कर्मफलहेतुर्भुर्मा ते संगोऽस्त्वकर्मणि ।।47।।
अध्याय 2

(Your right is to work only, but never to the fruit thereof. Let not the fruit of action be your object, nor let your attachment be to inaction.)

Sai Baba's advice was also on the same lines. When Annasaheb Dabholkar sought Baba's permission through Shama (Madhavrao Deshpande) to write Baba's life-history, Baba said : "He is only an outward instrument. I should myself write my life and satisfy the wishes of my devotees. He should get rid of his ego (doership), place (surrender) it at my feet. He who acts like this in life, him I help most."

— Chapter 2, p. 6

Similarly at Rajahmundry (Andhra Pradesh) on the banks of the Godavari river, a coconut given by Shri Vasudevananda Saraswati (Tembe Swami) for Shri Sai Baba, was inadvertently broken and eaten on the way by Pundalikarao of Nanded. When Pundalikarao realised his blunder, he was greatly perturbed and sad considering himself to have committed a great sin. What Sai Baba said to him was : "It was on account of My wish that the coconut was entrusted to you and ultimately broken on the way. Why should you take the doership of the actions on you ? Do not entertain the sense of doership in doing good as well as bad deeds: be entirely prideless and egoless in all things and thus your spiritual progress will be rapid."

— Chapter 50, p. 269

Hemadpant says in the original Marathi *Shri Sai Satcharita* : "While commencing an act, if the holy feet of one's *Sadguru* are remembered and the act is performed sincerely and honestly, the *Sadguru* will remove all barriers of the devotee regarding its success. One who believes that he himself will do the act but leave the results to the discretion of the *Sadguru*/God, will certainly accomplish the task."

— Chapter 48, Verses 43 and 44

This is what is known as '*Karma-Yoga*' which means a special skill of performing an act (कर्मसु कौशलम् — *Gita* ch. 2/ 50) which, when acquired, the act will not affect the person like water on the lotus leaf.

7

HUMAN BIRTHS

According to Hindu scriptures, there are 84 lakh types of births in this world (20 lakh trees and plants, 9 lakh aquatic animals, 11 lakh worms and insects, 10 lakh birds, 30 lakh beasts and 4 lakh human beings). The souls go on taking births and rebirths in these various types according to the merits and demerits of their previous lives. However, by chance, when their merits and demerits almost balance each other, they are born as human beings and given a chance to work out their salvation.

Four things are common to all the creatures, viz, food, sleep, fear and sex. In the case of man, he is endowed with a special faculty — knowledge — with the help of which he can attain self-realisation and deliverance from the cycle of rebirths, which is impossible in other types of births.

Sai Baba, therefore, advised his devotees not to waste this rare opportunity by indulging in satisfaction of senses only. According to him such a person would be no more than a beast without horns !

Sai Baba, therefore, liked those persons very much who took real interest in spiritual matters, and he removed all their difficulties and made them happy. In Chapter 41, we see how Sai Baba removed all obstacles in the way of Balkrishna Dev for his daily reading of the *Jnaneshwari* and even guided him in the matter by appearing in a dream.

Sai Baba used to complain : "Many people come to me and ask for wealth, health, power, honour, position, cure of diseases and other temporal matters. Rare is the person who comes here to Me and asks *Brahma Jnana* (self-realisation)"

— *Chapter 16, p. 88*

Therefore, Sai Baba used to bring such persons to Shirdi forcibly and, using various methods, lead them towards a proper spiritual life. He used to say : "Let my man be at any distance, a thousand *cos* away from me, he will be drawn to Shirdi like a sparrow with a thread tied to its feet."

— *Chapter 28, p. 150*

1) When Nanasaheb Chandorkar was Personal Secretary to the Collector of Ahmednagar, Sai Baba brought him to Shirdi by sending him messages not once but three times through Appa Kulkarni, the village Accountant. Later we know how Chandorkar became one of the dearest devotees of Sai Baba, who constantly and carefully looked after his spiritual and temporal interest.

2) Sai Baba appeared in Lala Lakhamichand's and Ramlal Punjabi's dreams and brought them to Shirdi.

3) Sai Baba demanded *khichadi* (rice cooked with dal and salt) from the lady from Barhanpur, in a dream and inspired her and her husband to visit Shirdi to fulfil that demand.

Some persons had given up worshipping their family idols or saints. Sai Baba made them visit Shirdi and reminded them of their previous worships and led them to spiritual paths again. Some examples are :

1) The father of Bhagvantrao was a devotee of Vithoba (Lord Krishna) of Pandharpur and used to visit the place every year regularly. He also used to worship Vithoba's idol in the house daily. After the father's death, the visit to

Pandharpur as well as the worship in the house had stopped. When Bhagvantrao visited Shirdi, Sai Baba pointed his finger towards him and said, "His father was my friend. I have brought him here because he does not offer me *naivedya* and keeps Me hungry. I shall now make him continue the worship."

2) Rao Bahadur Pradhan of Santa Cruz had received *Gurumantra* from his family Guru, Haribua, but he was neglecting the repetition of that *mantra.* Once Sai Baba was cooking food in a *handi* (pot) to feed poor people in the open space in front of the masjid. He did not allow anyone to come near him, but he did not mind Pradhan and Chandorkar's two young sons coming to him. At that time, Sai Baba was in a very pleasant mood and appeared to be singing aloud something. When Pradhan listened carefully, he heard, "What should we repeat? *Shri Rama Jaya Rama Jaya Jaya Rama*". On hearing these words Pradhan was at once reminded of the *Guru mantra* given to him by his family Guru. Pradhan was overcome with emotion and fell at Baba's feet with tears of regret. From then onwards Pradhan naturally started repeating that *mantra* regularly.

3) The son of Harishchandra Pitale was suffering from epilepsy. Pitale tried many allopathic and ayurvedic treatments but there was no cure. Ultimately on listening to Das Ganu's *kirtans,* Pitale took his son to Shirdi and surprisingly his son was cured merely with Baba's glances and application of his *udi.* When Pitale was returning, Baba gave him three rupees and reminding him about the two rupees given to him by Akkalkot Swamy earlier, persuaded Pitale to start the worship of Akkalkot Swamy again.

In some cases Sai Baba used force and even used his miraculous power to lead or relead persons towards the spiritual life :

1) Shama, alias Madhavrao Deshpande, was the closest and dearest devotee-cum-companion of Sai Baba. No wonder, therefore, that Sai Baba was keenly interested in his spiritual welfare. In Chapter 26, we can see, how in order to make Shama learn and recite the famous *Vishnu Sahasranama Stotra*, Sai Baba told a lie to Ramdasi that he had intense pain in the stomach, and asking him to go to the bazaar to buy 'Sona-mukhi' (a purgative drug) he stole Ramdasi's book and gave it to Shama in spite of Shama's unwillingness to accept it. Shama thought that Baba wanted to set him against Ramdasi by this act, but he had no idea that Baba wanted to tie this necklace of *Vishnu Sahasranama* round the neck of Shama to save him from the miseries of worldly existence. The efficacy of God's name is well known. It saves one from the sins and bad tendencies and frees one from the cycle of births and deaths. There is no easier *sadhana* than this.

2) Balasaheb, alias Purushottam Sakharam Bhate, at college was a free thinker, a free smoker, a veritable *Charvaka* whose creed may be summed up as 'Eat, drink and be merry today, for tomorrow we die.' He became *Mamlatdar* and was a very efficient officer much liked by his Collector. He was *Mamalatdar* of Kopargaon for about five years (1904 - 1909). All that time, he was scoffing at his educated friends (who met him on their way to Shirdi) for having any respect for Sai whom Bhate described as 'a madman'. The friends asked him to see Sai Baba just once and then form his judgement. In 1909, Bhate camped at Shirdi and saw Sai Baba every day. On the fifth day, Sai Baba covered him with a red garment usually worn by ascetics. From that day, Bhate was a changed man. He did not care for earnings or work; he only wished to be at Shirdi to serve Sai Baba, to live and die in his presence. Sai Baba asked his friend Dixit to draw up an application for leave for one year and Bhate's signature

was taken on it. The Collector gave him one year's time to see if he would return to his old self. But at the end of one year, Bhate still continued to be 'mad after his Guru' and was granted compassionate pension of about 30 rupees as one affected with 'religious melancholia'.

Bhate then lived at Shirdi with his wife and family attending to his *Nitya-Karma* and *Upanishad* reading, etc, before Sai (who would occasionally offer his remarks on that reading). He had the great honour of performing the last funeral rites of Sai Baba after his *Mahasamadhi*. No wonder then that Hemadpant, in his original Marathi *Shri Sai Satcharita*, describes Bhate as *Bhakta Ratna* (a jewel amongst devotees).

3) Das Ganu, alias Ganesh Dattatreya Sahasrabudhe, was serving in the Police department and was fond of composing 'Lavani', ie, lewd songs in Marathi for village dramas known as *tamashas* in Maharashtra. Initially Das Ganu had no faith in Sai Baba whom he visited in 1894 as a constable on duty along with Nanasaheb Chandorkar, then Personal Secretary to the Collector of Ahmednagar. But Sai Baba slowly drew Das Ganu towards himself and not only forced him to give up his police job but relieving him of all his vices, ultimately transformed him into a saint worthy of respect from thousands of disciples in his later life.

At the inspiration of Sai Baba, Das Ganu wrote three volumes of biographies on modern saints. Later he also wrote a number of other books (all in Ovi metre in Marathi) on spiritual subjects and was designated as *Sant-Kavi* (a poet-saint). Das Ganu also became a great *kirtankar* (narrator of religious stories and discourses in music) and was responsible for spreading Sai devotion, especially in Bombay and on the west coast of Maharashtra. He passed away in 1962 on a very auspicious day at the ripe age of 95 years.

4) Upasani Maharaj of Sakori, alias Kashinath Govind Upasani, had made quite good progress in *yoga* and spiritual *sadhana* before he came to Shirdi. But due to some mistakes that he had committed, he became ill and his progress was stopped. When he visited Shirdi, Baba did not allow him to go back, instead using his miraculous powers and by making him stay continuously for 4 years in Khandoba Temple which gave him various experiences, Sai Baba lead him to a very high spiritual status. After Sai Baba's *Mahasamadhi*, Upasani, at one time, was so much venerated that even Mahatma Gandhi approached him to seek his blessings for national welfare, and while at Bombay the devotees' line to get Upasani's *darshan* lasted one whole day and night. Upasani's Kanya Kumari Ashram at Sakori is also well known.

Sai Baba has continued this task of helping spiritual aspirants to reach their ultimate goal even after his *Mahasamadhi*. A conspicuous example of this is that of Shri Mota, a well known saint of Gujarat who left this world in 1976. Shri Mota already had spiritual guidance and favour from Dhuniwale Dada Sankheda in Madhya Pradesh. However, in 1938 (20 years after Sai Baba's *Mahasamadhi*), Sai Baba appeared before Mota a number of times at Karachi (now in Pakistan) and by teaching him certain yogic practices and by giving him several supernatural visions led him rapidly forward spiritually. Ultimately on 29 March 1939 at Kashi (Varanasi) on Ramanavami Day, Sai Baba gave Mota the great experience of non-duality and made as a self-realised soul forever. Shri Mota afterwards used to gratefully say, "Sai Baba gave final touches to my spiritual progress." Mota also composed a beautiful hymn of 17 stanzas in Gujarati language in praise of Sai Baba.

Thus during his lifetime as well as even afterwards, Sai Baba always tried to advise his devotees to make best use of the opportunity of human birth and achieve self-realisation. At the same time, he also warned his devotees not to neglect their bodies by hard penance and continuous fasts beyond their capacity : "The body should neither be neglected nor fondled but should be properly cared for just as a traveller on horse back takes care of his pony on the way till he reaches his destination and returns home."

— *Chapter 8, p. 46*

8

PLEASURES OF THE SENSES

In the case of Sai Baba there was no question of pursuit of pleasure of the senses: "Even though Sai Baba appeared to be tasting things with his tongue, he was not aware as to what he tasted nor had he any desire to enjoy that taste. Those who have no desire to enjoy the pleasure of the senses, will they ever enjoy them? The objects of the senses (hearing, touch, sight, taste and smell) do not even touch their organs. So will they ever get entangled in them?"

"Sai Baba's celibacy or absence from sexual pleasures was also remarkable, like Hanuman of the *Ramayana*. His sex organ was good for nothing like the teat hanging from the goat - only fit for passing urine."

Shri Sai Satcharita (Chapter 10, Ovis 96-101)

In *Shri Sai Satcharita*, dangers of pleasures of the senses have been described at various places. In Chapter 47 Hemadpant says : "This craving for the pleasures of the senses is very dangerous. It ultimately destroys the person craving for them. The deer dies because of its craving for sound, the cobra on account of wearing a beautiful jewel on its head, and the moth on account of its love for bright light. Such is the company of the senses. For enjoyment of the pleasures of the senses, money is required and while endeavouring to procure money, the craving for the senses increases more and more which then becomes irresistible." (Ovis 121-123)

Lord Krishna in the *Bhagavad Gita* says the same thing:

ध्यायतो पिष्यान्पुंसः संगस्तेषूपजायते।

संगात्संजायते कामः कामात्क्रोधो ड भिजायते ।।६२।।

क्रोधाभ्दवति संमोहः संमोहात्स्मृतिविभ्रमः ।

समृति भ्रंशाबुध्दिनाशो बुध्दिनाशात्प्रणश्यति ।।६३।।

— अध्याय 2

(The person dwelling on sense objects develops attachment for them. From attachment springs desire and from desire — unfulfilled — ensues anger.)

(From anger ensues infatuation, from infatuation, confusion of memory, loss of reason, and from loss of reason one goes to complete ruin.)

Lord Krishna also advises how to control the senses by giving example of a tortoise :

यदा संहरते चायं कूर्मो ड ड्गानीव सर्वशः।

इंद्रियाणीन्द्रियार्थेभ्यास्तस्य प्रज्ञा प्रतिष्ठिता ।।५८।।

— अध्याय 2

(When like the tortoise withdraws its limbs from all directions, he withdraws his senses from the sense objects, his mind becomes stable.)

The above is for those seeking self-realisation who with great efforts avoid the pleasures of the senses and achieve their goal of self-realisation. But what about the common family man who is constantly in close touch with these pleasures and is usually of a weak mind? How should he avoid the above-mentioned dangers? Should he give up his family life altogether ?

Shri Sai Baba never advised this. On the contrary, once when Nanasaheb Chandorkar, having been fed up with his family life, came to Baba for permission to leave it, Baba said to him: "Your complaint is correct, but worldly cares

are unavoidable till the body exists. Nobody can escape them
— even an ascetic has to worry about his loin cloth and
daily food. Look ! Even I am involved in the worldly cares
of my devotees" (pp. 91-92, Chapter 32, *Bhakta Leelamrit*
by Das Ganu) and then advised Chandorkar how to behave
while leading a family life. In *Shri Sai Satcharita* also Sai
Baba has narrated various simple methods to achieve welfare
without getting entangled in the pleasures of the senses and
without following immoral means.

1) Once when Nanasaheb Chandorkar was sitting in
front of Baba in Dwarkamai, a wealthy Mohammedan came
for Baba's *darshan* with his family. One of the ladies, while
saluting Baba's feet, removed her veil. Nanasaheb, who saw
her face, was so much smitten with her beauty that he was
tempted to see her face again and again. But Nana was
hesitating because of Baba and other devotees' presence.
Knowing Nana's restlessness Baba spoke to him, after the
lady had left the place, as follows: "Nana ! Why are you
getting agitated in vain? Let the senses do their allotted work
or duty. We should not meddle with their work. God has
created this beautiful world and it is our duty to appreciate
its beauty. The mind will get steady and calm slowly and
gradually. When the front door is open, why go by the back
one? When the heart is pure, there is no difficulty
whatsoever. Why should one be afraid of anyone if there is
no evil thought in us? The eyes may do their work, why
should you feel shy and tottering?"

— *Chapter 49, p. 263*

"Our mind is fickle by nature, It should not be allowed
to get wild. The senses may get restless, the body however
should be held in check and not allowed to be impatient.
Senses run after objects, but we should not follow them and

crave for their objects. By slow and gradual practice, restlessness can be conquered."

— *Chapter 49, pp. 263-264*

2) By teasing Hemadpant on locating some grains of gram on the latter's coat-sleeve, Sai Baba taught him and others another useful method of controlling one's senses : "Before the senses, mind and intellect enjoy their objects, Baba should first be remembered and if this be done, it is in a way an offering to him. The senses, etc, can never remain without their objects, but if these objects are first offered to the guru, the attachment for them will naturally vanish."

— *Chapter 24, p. 128*

To this Hemadpant himself adds: "When before enjoyment of the objects, you think that Baba is close by or present, the question whether the object is fit to be enjoyed or not will at once arise. Then the object that is not fit to be enjoyed will be shunned and in that way, our vicious habits or vices will disappear and our character will improve."

— *Chapter 24, p. 128*

3) Better than these, in Chapter 20, we see that through Kakasaheb Dixit's maidservant, Baba has taught us a beautiful and ingenious method of enjoying sense objects. The maidservant was always cheerful and contented, even when on the first day she had only a torn rag on her person, or the next day when she wore a new saree presented by M. V. Pradhan or on the third day when she wore the torn rag again. In fact the maidservant thus gave a practical demonstration of the lesson of the *Ishavasya Upanishad* :

ईशा वास्यामिदं सर्वं, यत्किंच जगत्यां जगत् ।
तेन त्यक्तेन भुञ्जीथा, मा गृध्दः कस्य स्विद्धनम् ।।1।।

(All this movable and immovable that exists in this universe is pervaded by Lord. Remembering Him, thou should enjoy whatever is bestowed by him, without coveting anybody's wealth.)

Thus Sai Baba has given us many simple methods to control the senses without giving up our family life. However, to the person seeking self-realisation he insists on strict discipline.

He says : "Objects of senses are harmful. With *Viveka* (discrimination) as our charioteer, we will control the mind and will not allow the senses to go astray. With such a charioteer we reach the *Vishnupada* — the final abode, our real home from which there is no return."

— *Chapter 49, p. 264*

'MAYA'

There are three meanings of the word *Maya*. The first meaning is 'the formative energy of *Brahman* or the Supreme Spirit considered as the cause of the universe.' The second meaning is 'the illusion by virtue of which one the unreal universe is considered as really existent and as distinct from the Supreme Spirit', and the third meaning is 'enchantment or fondness for the material world and its contents'.

Creative Energy of Brahman

In mythology *Maya* is personified as a female and the consort of *Brahman* or the Supreme Spirit. She is made of three qualities (*Satva* — goodness or purity, *Rajas* — activity/passion, and *Tamas* — illusion/ignorance), and is normally invisible and one with the Supreme Being. On becoming visible, she forms the universe. We are not directly concerned with this aspect of *Maya*. Only being awed with her great power and oneness with the Supreme Spirit, we adore, bow and celebrate her festivals during *Navaratra*, the first nine days of the bright halves of *Chaitra* and *Ashwin* (months of the Hindu calendar).

Power of Illusion

This *Maya* or illusion is very powerful. Sai Baba himself talks about her in the *Shri Sai Satcharita* as follows: "Even though I have become an ascetic and am sitting at one place avoiding all worries, Maya troubles Me again and again. She is the ancient Maya of Hari (Lord Vishnu) and confounds even great personalities like Brahma (the first of the Hindu Trinity). How can then a weak-minded fakir like Me escape her powerful effect?"

— Chapter 18, Verses 4 to 6

Why should we have to try to escape from this *Maya's* clutches? Because on account of her, we get a wrong idea about this world and also about ourselves — just as in semi-darkness, we mistake a rope for a serpent. Then considering this world as real and our body as our soul, we indulge in worldly pleasures and get caught in the rotation of births and deaths. How then should one get rid of this illusion or misunderstanding and its consequences? The only method is to get the true knowledge of this world and of ourselves from the *Sadguru* (spiritual preceptor). If this is not possible, then the next simple method is to practise devotion to God. The devotees do not have to worry. *Maya* will not trouble them.

Enchantment or Fondness

The average person is intimately concerned with this meaning of *Maya*. In the material world, even though knowing that his wife, children, property, wealth, etc, are not permanent and will not accompany him after death, a person is enchanted with them and consequently becomes unhappy.

In this connection, the story of King Surath and the tradesman Samadhi narrated in *Shri Durga Saptashati*

(Seven hundred verses in praise of Goddess Durga) is interesting. In the dynasty of Chaitra, there was a king named Surath, who used to look after his subjects like his own children. Unfortunately he was defeated in a war with Kolvidhvansis, and his capital city was attacked by the enemies. Taking advantage of this, his wicked ministers looted his treasury and took charge of his armed forces. So, Surath escaped from his capital under the pretext of going for hunting and entered a thick forest. While thus wandering in the forest, he saw Sage Medha's hermitage, where he was received quite well. After spending some days in that holy atmosphere, one day he became agitated on account of attachment to his previous belongings and remembering past incidents of his life, and he started worrying. Thinking that his dear elephant, other beautiful things and the treasury collected with great efforts must be in a state of utter destruction, he became very unhappy. He also thought that the new king may be harassing his subjects. Then wandering in the hermitage in such a condition, he came across a tradesman named Samadhi.

He asked him, "Who are you? Why have you come here in this hermitage? You seem to be in a great worry."

The tradesman replied, "Oh King Surath! I am a tradesman by caste and my name is Samadhi. I was born in a rich family. I grew up and earned lots of money. I got married and had children also, but on becoming old my wife and children ruthlessly drove me out of the house. My relatives have robbed my wealth. That is why I am worried about my family. In my absence, are my wife and children faring well? I hope they do not have to work extra hard and my children have not taken to ill paths. These and other matters are worrying me."

Then the king asked him, "Shethji! How is it that you are so fond of your wife and children who have driven you out of the house?"

Thereupon the tradesman replied, "Oh king! What you say is quite correct. Even knowing that they do not love me, I cannot be harsh to them. I do not know why!"

Then, in order to solve this problem, King Surath and Samadhi went to Sage Medha to seek his opinion. The sage said, "Sentiment of affection is equally common both to human beings and beasts or birds also. Although troubled with hunger themselves, see how the birds out of infatuation feed their little ones! Similarly, human beings, though more intelligent, are seen expecting their favours to be gratefully repaid by their children. Although these beings are aware of its futility, they, because of the powers of this *Mahamaya*, are trapped into this whirlpool of infatuation. One should not therefore be surprised at this.

महामाया हरेश्वेषा तया संमोहयते जगत्।
ज्ञानि नामणि चेतांसि देवी भगवती सा ।।55।।
सा विद्या परमा मुक्तेर्हेतुभूता सनातनी ।।57।।
संसारबन्धहेतुश्व सैव सर्वेश्वरेश्वरी ।।58।।

– श्री दुर्गासप्तशती अध्याय 1

(This world is infatuated because of Goddess Mahamaya of Vishnu. She makes the minds of even the most wise persons entangle in her mad enchantments. If she is pleased she bestows freedom from rebirths. She is the ancient and highest knowledge, the cause of entanglement as well as escape from worldly life and the Goddess of all Gods.)

Even then, one must try to get out of this infatuation of worldly life. In *Shri Sai Satcharita* in Chapters 17 and 23, this is beautifully explained by comparing the personal soul in the human body with the parrot finding great happiness in binding itself on a rod in a golden cage and getting red chillies and pomegranate grains ready to eat without effort. He is advised to escape out of the cage and enjoy the freedom of flying anywhere and enjoying any number of guavas and pomegranates in the gardens.

In the end, what Baba advises us time and again in this respect is : "The mundane life is fickle like lightning in the clouds. There the moments of happiness are very rare. Mother, father, sister, husband, wife, son, daughter and uncle — all of them are like logs of wood flowing in a river. They appear to be together for a moment and then suddenly due to an oncoming wave, get separated never to be rejoined again."

— Chapter 24, Verses 21-23

"The moment a person is born he starts moving on the road to death. Hence a person who believes in doing anything tomorrow or the day after, has lost the opportunity. Always remember that death is around and the body is prey to death anytime. Such is the mundane life. So always be cautious."

— Chapter 24, Verses 25-26

"This skeleton or frame of the body is made up of skin, flesh, blood and bones, an encumbrance in the path of attainment of self-realisation or emancipation. So give up fondness for the same. Do not idolise or give too much importance to it. Treat it as a servant only. By constantly patting it do not make it a door to hell. Give it food and clothes and attention just enough for sustenance and use it for attaining spiritual progress and release from the bonds of births and deaths."

— Chapter 8, Verses 33-34

"Because of great luck and in return for many meritorious acts, you have attained this human birth. So make good use of it every moment. Before the body falls dead, work hard to get self-realisation. Do not waste a single moment of human life."

— *Chapter 8, Verses 41 and 78*

And most important : "Catch the feet of *Sadguru* to get out of the clutches of *Maya*. Seek His refuge exclusively and you will get rid of the fear of another birth or further migration. Let the inevitable death come, but let us not forget Hari (Lord Krishna). With senses perform the duties laid down for the period of your life (*ashram*) by scriptures and with mind think of the Lords's feet."

— *Chapter 39, Verses 82-83*

10

EGOTISM

Egotism means overwhelming opinion of oneself, pretentious display or arrogance. Sai Baba was absolutely against this trait and advised his devotees to observe humility in this world.

"My dear devotees! If the wealth comes to you, be very humble like the trees loaded with fruits." (71)

"Always respect holy and virtuous persons and saints and bend before them like grass before wind." (72)

"Do not forget that opulence is transitory like the afternoon shade. Therefore do not harass anybody, being intoxicated due to riches." (73)

- Das Ganu's *Arwachin Bhakta Leelamrit*, Chapter 32

When Shri Dabholkar asked Sai Baba's permission through Shama to write Baba's biography, Baba told him the same thing — to give up conceit and false pride : "He is only an outward instrument. I should write Myself My life and satisfy the wishes of My devotees. He should get rid of his ego, place (or surrender) it at My feet. He who acts like this in life, him I help most."

— *Chapter 2, p. 6*

Sai Baba behaved according to his preachings. Many devotees, during Sai Baba's time as well as today, believe him to be an incarnation of God. But Sai Baba himself never said, 'I am God'; on the contrary he used to call himself 'an humble servant of God' who remembered Him and always uttered *Allah Malik hai* (God is the sole Proprietor or Owner).

Later on, as people became aware of Baba's greatness, they started flocking to him from long distances bringing with them flowers, fruits and *dakshina* (cash offerings) and tried to worship him. To start with, Baba resisted this and getting angry sometimes even threw away their dishes containing such articles. But later on, realising the devotees' loving persistence, allowed them to do so.

When close and well-to-do devotees like Nanasaheb Chandorkar and Kakasaheb Dixit tried to fix stone slabs in the masjid or construct a shade in front of it, Baba used to get wild with anger and pull out the iron pillars recently fixed! For the *chavadi* procession, Radhakrishna Mai secured a palanquin for Baba, but he never sat in it, preferring to walk all the way. Both Hindus and Muslims came to him, but he never bothered whether they bowed to him in respect or not. Once a person named Nana Wali approached Baba and said, "Get up! I am going to sit on your *gaddi* (mattress)." Without showing any displeasure, Baba immediately got up and allowed Nana Wali to do so. No wonder that Nana Wali, in a minute, left the seat and bowing respectfully to Baba, requested him to resume the seat again.

Sai Baba possessed great yogic and divine powers, by using which he used to help his devotees to get rid of severe diseases or difficulties. He helped Dr Pillay in getting rid of guinea worms on his legs (Chapter 34), he cured Bhimaji Patil's tuberculosis (Chapter 13) and by taking the form of a tonga driver he took the *udi* and *arati* urgently to far-off Jamner to save Nanasaheb Chandorkar's daughter Mainatai from delivery pains. But Baba never accepted the doership of these acts of his.

In Chapter 34, see what he said to Shama : "Though I do nothing, they hold Me responsible for the actions which take place on account of destiny. I am only their witness. The Lord is the sole Doer and Inspirer. He is also most merciful. I am neither God nor Lord. I am His obedient servant and remember Him often."

— *Chapter 34, p. 191*

Sai Baba not only did not take the credit or helping his devotees, but he expressed gratefulness to them for giving him an opportunity to help them. Here is a specimen.

Baba once spoke very humbly as follows: "Slave of slaves, I am your debtor. I am satisfied with your *darshan*. It is a great favour that I saw your feet. I am an insect in your excreta. I consider blessed thereby."

— *Chapter 10, pp. 61-62*

What great humility!

This is in everyday mundane life. But for attainment of self-realisation also, Baba advised his devotees repeatedly to give up ego or conceit.

Once Jawar Ali, a learned *Moulvi*, came to Shirdi (1880-1890 probably) and asked Sai Baba to become his disciple and accompany him to Rahata. At that time Baba himself had a number of devotees revering and worshiping him. Without any hesitation, Baba accompanied him to Rahata and stayed there for 2-3 months serving him until the Shirdi devotees brought him back with great difficulty. Thus Baba showed by actual conduct how one should get rid of one's ego and perform the duties of a disciple to attain the highest goal of self-realisation.

Sai Baba once described how he was successful in his quest of God because of his humbleness in accepting the advice and loaf of bread offered by a *banjarin* in the forest. Baba also narrated how by surrendering himself to his Guru completely, he attained self-realisation : "My Guru became all-in-all. My home and property, mother and father, everything. All My senses left their places and concentrated themselves in My eyes, and My sight was centred on him. This was My Guru — the sole object of My meditation. I was conscious of none else... By his grace, realisation flashed upon Me by itself without effort or study."

— *Chapter 32, pp. 175-176*

When Pundalikrao of Nanded felt very guilty about breaking and using the coconut given to him by Shri Vasudevanand Saraswati, alias Tembye Swami, meant for Sai Baba, the great being answered thus: "You need not worry yourself any more about the matter. It was on account of My wish that the coconut was entrusted to you and ultimately broken on the way. Why should you take the doership of the actions on you? Do not entertain the sense of doership in doing good as well as bad deeds, be entirely prideless and egoless in all things and thus your progress will be rapid."

— *Chapter 50, pp. 268-269*

What a beautiful spiritual instruction Baba gave!

Thus whether in everyday mundane life or during efforts for self-realisation, Sai Baba stressed the need for giving up egotism and adopting humility. No wonder, therefore, that Hemadpant, in *Shri Sai Satcharita*, while describing an ideal devotee, says : "One who has regard for his body, does not deserve the epithet 'devotee'. One who is absolutely without egotism, possesses real devotion. One who is arrogant due to learning and one who has undeserved pride of his greatness is the centre of religious hypocrisy."

— *Chapter 49, Verses 13-14*

NON-VIOLENCE

Non-violence means not to harm anybody physically, verbally and mentally.

अहिंसा परमो धर्म: (Non-violence is the greatest religion) is a famous maxim. In *Manusmriti* (conduct of rules laid down by Manu, the greatest legislator of Hindu religion) also, non-violence has been given the first place:

अहिंसा सत्यमस्तेय शौचमिंदियनिग्रह: ।
एवं सामासिकं धर्म चातुर्वण्ये ड ब्रवीन्मनु: ।।६३।।

– अध्याय 10

(Non-violence, truth, non-stealing, purity and restraint of senses are, in brief, rules of good conduct for all the four castes, viz, priests, warriors, traders and menials alike.)

Sai Baba also encouraged the principle of non-violence. But his method was very practical. For instance, to those persons who have been permitted by their religion/castes or who have been eating non-vegetarian food for generations, Sai Baba did not tell them to give it up. Sai Baba himself dressed like a Muslim fakir and lived in a masjid. So to suit his appearance, he had no objection in tasting non-vegetarian food. Not only this, but sometimes he even cooked non-vegetarian food and distributed it among the poor. However, he ensured that non-vegetarian food was given only to those who ate it and to others he never offered it nor tempted or forced them to eat it.

Sai Baba was very humorous by nature and hence joked with his devotees/visitors about their hatred for non-vegetarian food. Once, on *ekadashi* day (11th day of a fortnight in the Hindu calendar considered to be very holy), Baba asked a very religious Brahmin Dada Kelkar, to go and buy mutton from the market. But when Dada Kelkar, like a true disciple, started to go, Baba stopped him.

Similarly, once a poor brahmin came to meet Sai Baba, hoping to get some cash from him. At that time some boys were mincing meat for cooking. Baba asked one of the boys to put some pieces in the brahmin's bag. The brahmin was very angry but could not say anything out of fear. On the way back to his village, when he came across a canal of water, he threw away the pieces of meat in a field and dipping the cloth in the canal water started washing it. At that time, he felt some hard stuff sticking to the cloth which he thought maybe a piece of bone. But on close inspection, he was surprised to find it to be a piece of shining gold. Immediately the brahmin ran to the field where he had thrown away the rest of the meat pieces. But he found nothing there and so cursed his bad luck and felt angry with the non-vegetarian Baba.

In Sai Baba's time, brahmins used to think that not to eat non-vegetarian food was the prime means of attaining spiritual progress and hence used to look down upon those eating non-vegetarian food. Baba perhaps wanted to teach them that the real means of attaining spiritual progress was not just avoiding non-vegetarian food but in obeying Guru's (spiritual preceptor's) orders faithfully and without hesitation, and also accepting anything given by a saint humbly and respectfully. Sai Baba was probably right in his view, since if eating non-vegetarian-food was really an obstacle to spiritual progress, great seers like Prophet Mohammed of Islam or Jesus Christ of Christianity who ate them, would not have attained self-realisation.

Therefore, Sai Baba propagated non-violence in its real sense. Notice his following words of advice : "If any men or creatures come to you, do not discourteously drive them away, but receive them well and treat them with real respect. Shri Hari (God) will be certainly pleased if you give water to the thirsty, bread to the hungry, clothes to the naked and your verandah to strangers for sitting and resting. If anybody wants money from you and you are not inclined to give, do not give, but do not bark at him like a dog."

— *Chapter 19, p. 101*

"Let anybody speak hundreds of things against you, do not resent it by giving any bitter reply. If you tolerate such things, you will be certainly happy."

— *Chapter 19, pp. 101-102*

"He who carps and cavils at others, pierces Me in the heart and injures Me, but he that suffers and endures, pleases Me most."

— *Chapter 44, p. 240*

Quite correct! Speaking harsh words are more piercing and worse than sharp arrows, which can never be pulled back.

Sai Baba's love for beasts and birds is well known. Every day, after returning from his begging schedule, Sai Baba used to put whatever he had collected as alms in his bag in an earthen pot in the masjid, and dogs, cats and cows were free to partake of it as much as they liked. Sai Baba never drove them away. Similarly Baba complimented Mrs Tarkhad for feeding a hungry dog with a piece of bread. "Every act like this, will stand you in good stead. Sitting in this masjid, I shall never, never speak untruth. Take pity on Me like this. First give bread to the hungry and then eat yourself."

— Chapter 9, p. 55

Once in 1917, a small dog, bitten by a rabid dog, began to chase big dogs. The villagers, clubs in hand, then chased the small dog. It ran through the streets and finally got into Dwarkamai, stood behind Baba and made him its sanctuary.

"Villagers : Baba, that dog is mad. Drive it out and we will kill it.

Baba : You mad fellows, you get out. Do you want to persecute and kill a poor creature?"

Thus Baba saved the life of that dog and it proved to be not rabid.

Sai Baba preached non-violence even in the case of poisonous creatures like scorpions and serpents. For instance (Chapter 22), he replied when Hemadpant asked for Baba's opinion on whether poisonous creatures should be killed or not : "God lives in all beings and creatures, whether they be serpents or scorpions. He is the great wire-puller of the world and all beings: serpents, scorpions, etc, obey His command. Unless He wills it, nobody can do any harm to others. So we should take pity and love all creatures."

— Chapter 9, p. 55

Thus Baba's preaching regarding non-violence was unique and most infallible. He told his devotees that he or God Himself was in all creatures whether beasts or birds.

For instance, see what he said to Mrs Tarkhad : "The dog which you saw before meals and to which you gave a piece of bread, is one with Me. I am roaming in their forms. He who sees Me in all these creatures, is My beloved."

— *Chapter 9, p. 55*

No wonder that when Hemadpant was attending discourses on Ram Vijay by Kakasaheb Dixit, he found a scorpion sitting on the cloth over his shoulder; he did not kill it but taking it outside in a garden let it free. Similarly, when a cobra entered Bala Nevaskar's cowshed he did not get afraid but considering the cobra's arrival as that of Baba himself, brought a pot full of milk for it to drink.

Thus if devotees are once convinced that Baba resides in every creature, would they ever dare to touch non-vegetarian food in any form at all?

Another question arises: if Baba practised non-violence, how is it then that he frequently got into high temper, abused and chased his devotee raising his *sataka* (stick)? Well! This was necessary to stop people from disturbing him unnecessarily. It is rightly said : "An unpoisonous serpent should also raise its big hood. Whether poisonous or non-poisonous a raised hood is always very frightening." Thus Baba's anger was only for outward show, and in his heart-of-hearts, he loved his devotees.

Hemadpant remarks, "Though He seemed to shake with anger and His red eyes rolled round and round, still He was internally a stream of affection and motherly love. Immediately He called out to His devotees and said that He never knew that He was ever angry with His devotees: that if mothers kicked their children and if the sea turned back the rivers, only then He would neglect the devotees' welfare."

— *Chapter 11, Verse 73 to 75*

GOOD CONDUCT

Good conduct means thinking and behaving according to rules of behaviour laid down in the scriptures and generally accepted by the society. Sai Baba used to always say :

''जैसी जिसकी नियत, वैसी उसकी बरकत''

Niyat means the manner or intention of behaving in society. If one is honest and not deceiving anybody, then only a person will prosper and achieve success in life. To Rao Saheb Galvankar (son-in-law of Annasaheb Dabholkar), Baba had stressed two points by asking *dakshina* of two rupees — probity and integrity in behaviour and purity and chastity in sex. The *Manusmriti* (famous Hindu code of conduct) also describes good conduct as the greatest religion (आचारो परमो धर्मः)

For achieving emancipation (ie, the highest and most excellent end of man) purity of mind is very essential:

"Trying to achieve emancipation without achieving purity of mind is only waste of energy and a parade of one's knowledge."

— *Chapter 17, Verse 76*

Purity of mind cannot be achieved without purity of conduct. "Without performing deeds approved by scriptures, purity of mind is not possible and without purity of mind knowledge of *Brahman* (the Supreme Being considered as cause of the universe) is not possible."

— *Chapter 17, Verse 44*

"In this human birth, one should first behave as per rules laid down for your type, by which purity of mind will be achieved, resulting in the knowledge of *Brahman*."

— *Chapter 37, Verse 88*

Purity of mind is to be retained even after achieving knowledge of Brahman: "One who constantly performs vile acts forbidden by scriptures and one who does not understand what is beneficial and not beneficial to him, what is the use of his being endowed with knowledge of Brahman?" (25)

"And even after obtaining knowledge of Brahman, one who acts in violence of conduct rules, cannot stay here on this earth nor there in heaven but has to hang in between like Trishanku (a celebrated king of the Solar race who had to hang in between heaven and the earth as he was not accepted in either place). (49)

"Inwardly whose deeds are vile but outwardly who makes a show of being absorbed in contemplation of Brahman, whose actions are neglectful of prescribed rules of conduct and whose thinking also is corrupt, is certainly spiritually ignorant. (103)

— *Chapters 17, Verse 37 and 38*

To illustrate the importance of honest behaviour, the author of *Sri Sai Satcharita* narrates in Chapter 24 the story of Sudama (co-student of Krishna in Guru Sandipani's *ashram*) : "Once when Krishna and Balram had gone to the forest to collect firewood, the wife of Guru Sandipani sent some fried grams with Sudama for all of them to eat before drinking water. Later in the forest, when Krishna came to Sudama and said that he was thirsty, Sudama told him to rest as one should not drink water without eating something. Though Sudama had fried grams given by the wife of Guru Sandipani, he did not share them with Krishna.

When Krishna put his head on the lap of Sudama and slept, Sudama took out the grams and started eating them. Krishna listening to the noise of chewing the grams, woke up and asked Sudama what he was eating. Sudama lied to Krishna, saying, 'What is there to eat? I am shivering with cold, my teeth are rattling and I cannot even recite the *Vishnu Sahasranama Stotra.*" On hearing this, the omniscient Krishna said, "I just dreamt about a man eating something and when asked about this, he said. 'What earth (dust) should I eat?' (meaning he had nothing to eat)! The other man said, 'Let it be so.' Dada! This is only a dream. I know that you won't eat anything without me, under the influence of the dream I asked you what were you eating."

Had Sudama known even a bit about the omniscient Krishna and his *leela,* he would not have acted as he did. As a consequence, he had to pass his later life in utter poverty. But when he later offered Krishna a handful of parched rice, earned by his wife with her own labour, Krishna was pleased and gave him a golden mansion to stay in and immense wealth to enjoy.

That is why Sai Baba used to speak of persons with bad conduct in disgust and advise his devotees not to have anything to do with such persons: "Persons who say what is wrong if they behave as they like, are idiots. Those who do not follow the rules of good conduct should be avoided first." (78)

"If they are seen coming from the front, one should step aside and considering them very dangerous should not stand in their shadow, even if it results in extra trouble." (79)

— Chapter 3

13

BLISS (PERFECT JOY)

S ai Baba himself was bliss-incarnate. Hemadpant in
Shri Sai Satcharita says: "Sai Baba is a mine of blissful
nature—filled to the brim like the ocean. If the devotee is
lucky there will not be any dearth of great bliss for him."
— *Chapter 1, Verse 66*

"Sai Baba's condition was constantly merged with
Brahman or Absolute Reality and removed from the cares
and troubles of secular life. He was bliss-incarnate.
Listeners hear and scholars read in scriptures that Bliss is
Brahman but the devotees experience it in Shirdi itself."
— *Chapter 11, Verses 37-38*

Absolutely correct. Sai Baba's nature was gay and full
of frolic and fun. In his young days tying jingling bells to
his ankles, he used to dance and sing beautifully to the beats
of a small drum (tambourine). Although in a state of
contemplation, he used to watch the dances of *muralis*
(females dedicated to God Khandoba—an incarnation of
Shiva in Maharashtra) and nod his head in approval on
hearing their lyrical songs. He was also very fond of
lighting lamps (earthen receptacles of oil and wick) in
Dwarkamai and in temples, especially during the Diwali
festival.

Sai Baba was very fond of wit and humour. In Chapter
24, we see how he joked with Shri Dabholkar on finding

grains of soaked and parched grams in the folds of his coat-sleeve. Similarly, in the same chapter we come across Sai Baba enjoying a quarrel between Anna Chinchanikar and Maushi Bai and sorting it out by his timely and appropriate utterance, "Anna! What harm or impropriety is there if a child kisses its mother?"

Sai Baba had special relationship with Mhalsapati, an elderly devotee from the very day of Baba's arrival at Shirdi, and Tatya Kote Patil, the young son of Bayajabai who used to feed him in his early days. Both had the special privilege of sleeping with Baba in Dwarkamai, legs touching each other in the centre and heads pointing in three different directions. Then during the night sometimes Baba used to get up and place somebody's legs on somebody else's body and somebody else's legs on his own body. When in the morning Mhalsapati and Tatya would ask who did this, Baba used to laugh merrily. Tatya used to address Baba as Mama (maternal uncle). As a result of this there used to be bouts of fun between them. Another close companion of Sai Baba was Shama alias Madhavrao Deshpande. We have seen how Baba even pinched his cheek in fun (Chapter 36).

By this blissful nature, Sai Baba probably wanted to convey to people that in worldly life calamities and misfortunes are very common. Why should we then be unhappy and sullen by worrying over them? Why not be cheerful and laughing always? Listen to Baba's following words of advice: "From beginning to end, one should live one-pointedly in whatever condition decided by fate, and be contented. Never worry."

— Chapter 13, Verse 3

"Never worry a bit in life. Always be full of merriment. This was his advice."

— *Chapter 17, Verse 3*

Das Ganu Maharaj also quotes Baba's similar advice in his *Bhakti Leelamrit*: "A wise person should be happy in whatever condition he had to live as per his fate and never be restless."

— *Chapter 33, Verse 66*

When Anna Chinchanikar requested Baba to get Dabholkar another job after retirement, Baba said the same thing: "Let him now serve Me and he will be happy in his mundane life. His plates for meals will always be full and never empty in his lifetime. If he regularly serves Me devotedly all his problems will be solved."

— *Chapter 3, Verse 77*

Similarly, in Chapter 35, see what beautiful advice Baba gave indirectly to Thakkar Dharamsi, the proprietor of Kaka Mahajani's firm: "There was a fickle-minded gentleman. He had health and wealth and was free from both mental and physical afflictions. However, he took on himself needless anxieties and burdens and wandered hither and thither, thus losing his peace of mind. Sometimes he dropped the burdens and at other times carried them again. His mind knew no steadiness. Seeing his state, I took pity on him and said, 'Now, please keep your faith at any one place (point) you like. Why roam like this? Stick quietly to one place.'"

— *Chapter 35, pp. 195-196*

In short, Sai Baba's teaching was that one should always be satisfied and smiling in life. Similarly, while trying for final emancipation also, instead of getting involved in terms like "Merging in Brahman, etc," one should try to be always blissful in nature. Once this nature and condition is achieved, the mind will be full of happiness, peace and satisfaction, which is the highest achievement in life.

At this juncture somebody may question as to how then Sai Baba used to get wild with anger and even chase the devotees raising his stick (*sataka*). Yes! But this anger was always under control and in few minutes he would become normal again. In his heart he had great love for his devotees.

Hemadpant, the author of *Shri Sai Satcharita*, says in Chapter 11: "Though He seemed to shake with anger and His red eyes rolled round and round, still He was internally a stream of affection and motherly love. Immediately He called out to His devotees and said that He never knew that He was ever angry with His devotees: that if mothers kicked their children and if the sea turned back the rivers, only then He would neglect the devotees' welfare; that He, the slave of His devotees, always stood by them and responded to them whenever they called upon Him."

— Chapter 11, p. 65

In fact, Sai Baba's anger was only outward and feigned to ensure that people did not trouble him unnecessarily, taking him for granted. It is wisely said, "A non-poisonous snake also should raise its big hood, because whether poisonous or non-poisonous, show of hood is itself fearsome." However, for his devotees, his advice was to avoid anger (eg, his description of the previous life of two goats in Chapter 46 and those of the serpent and the frog in Chapter 47).

'NISHTHA' (FIRM FAITH)

There are two important words in Sai Baba's teachings, viz, *Nishtha* (firm faith or fixed devotion) and *Saburi* (patience or perseverence).

Firm faith means fixed devotion to one's favourite or tutelar deity or patron saint and convinced belief that he, being all powerful and conversant with our past, present and future, will always act for our ultimate welfare. Therefore, if a devotee of Shri Sai Baba, leaving all worries, decides to live cheerfully in whatever good or bad condition Baba decides to keep him, he will always get great happiness and peace of mind in this world. For instance, in Chapter 25, we see, Damuanna of Ahmednagar asking Baba's advice whether he should trade in cotton or not. When Baba said 'No', Damuanna was disappointed and even regretted asking for Baba's advice. But later when he learnt that his friends suffered a great loss in the deal, his faith in Baba increased immensely. No wonder therefore that great devotees like Kakasaheb Dixit and Bapusaheb Butty never did anything without consulting Baba: "Kakasaheb totally relied on Sai Baba. He would not do anything without consulting Baba first." (99)

"Because of this conviction he even rejected profits worth lakhs of rupees and stuck to this decision till death." (100)

— *Chapter 45*

"On getting any idea, Butty used to first consult Baba and without His consent never used to start any work." (150)

"This was his usual practice, without Baba's consent Butty never started to do anything." (151)

— *Chapter 39*

For achieving self-realisation especially, there is a great need for faith in a spiritual preceptor (*Sadguru*). The path of self-realisation is very difficult and painful. Therefore merciful guidance of an experienced preceptor is very essential. Our own cleverness or logic alone does not serve the purpose: "Here reasoning is of no use. Great respect for the preceptor is essential. There is no need to show smartness of intellect. Firm faith and trust in the spiritual preceptor is required." (228)

"Those who indulge in mere reasoning and conjecturing, discussing and debating or hypocritical examining do not receive advice from the saints properly. However one possessing firm faith gets it easily." (229)

— *Chapter 35*

"There is no place for a person skilled in the science of logic. He will rotate in the whirlpool of suspicion and doubt. Without sacred scriptures and spiritual preceptor, understanding or perception of the Supreme Spirit does not become steady." (122)

"Innumerable stars of one's own intellect cannot, but one Moon of sacred scriptures or spiritual preceptor only is sufficient to dispel the darkness of ignorance and to avoid 84 lakhs rounds of births and deaths." (123)

— *Chapter 16*

That is why Sai Baba used to tell his devotees repeatedly: "Too much cleverness is not of much use. One should listen to the advice of elders."

In this respect, Sai Baba has narrated his own experience in Chapter 32. After reading the scriptures and acquiring knowledge, four persons including Sai Baba set out in search of God. During the search, while in a forest, they met a *banjarin* (nomadic trader in salt, grains, etc) who advised them to eat some bread and take a guide with them. But they did not listen to him and started the search by themselves. As a result, in a short while, they lost their way and after wandering all over returned to the same place. The *banjarin* again said to them: "A guide is necessary during a big or small task. A search taken up on an empty stomach is never successful. Intellect has a tendency to wander away in innumerable directions." (56)

The other three rejected the offer again, Sai Baba however accepted and ate the piece of bread and water offered by the nomad. Then a miracle occurred. The spiritual preceptor suddenly appeared on the scene and promised to help in the search. Sai Baba went with him. The spiritual preceptor tied a rope to Sai Baba's feet, hung him upside down in a well full of water and tied the other end of the rope to the branch of a tree top and went away. But Sai Baba remained there quite happy with full trust in the preceptor. After 5-6 hours the preceptor returned, pulled Sai Baba out of the well and took him to his school for tutoring. Sai Baba described the stay as follows: "Worldly hopes and desires which are difficult to conquer were vanished and the chain obstructing the path leading to spiritual activities was broken. I desired to put my hands round the preceptor's neck and fix him in my eyes forever." (77)

"Without his reflection in my eye, I considered it as a round piece of flesh only and preferred to remain a blind person. Such was my condition in the school." (78)

What a great faith in the spiritual preceptor!

In Chapter 23 of *Shri Sai Satcharita*, there are a number of examples as to how faith in one's spiritual preceptor should be firm.

Once a student of yoga came to Shirdi with Nanasaheb Chandorkar to clear some of his doubts about *yoga*. On seeing Baba eating onion (which is taboo for yogis) with bread, he doubted Baba's ability to clear his doubts. But later on, experiencing Baba's powers of reading the other person's mind, he respectfully approached Baba and had his doubts satisfactorily cleared.

In another example, Shamrao Deshpande was bitten by a poisonous snake. The villagers tried to take him to Viroba (Shiva) temple for cure, but Shama rushed to Sai Baba, who instead of trying to cure him, shouted at him, "Don't come up. Get away from here." But Shama did not get disappointed and continued sitting outside on the steps of the masjid. Afterwards Baba cooled down and sent Shama home with assurance of cure, which indeed proved correct the following morning.

In the third example, Sai Baba ordered Kakasaheb Dixit (a pure brahmin) to kill a goat with a knife, and Kakasaheb Dixit, like a true and faithful devotee, immediately got ready to do so: "Your nectar-like words are dictates or *shastras* for us." (170)

"We do not know any other religious practice. We are not ashamed to say that obedience of Guru's words is the gist and sacred scripture for us." (171)

"We do not know violence or non-violence, our Guru's feet are our saviours. We do not discuss why particular order was given. We only know that our duty is to obey the order." (171)

"We, your disciples, only know how to obey your orders. If necessary, we will even sacrifice our lives but obey your orders." (181)

No wonder therefore that Sai Baba once promised Kakasaheb Dixit that he would carry him in an aeroplane, and afterwards, while talking about Baba with his co-disciple, Annasaheb Dabholkar, sitting on a bench in the suburban train of Bombay city, Kakasaheb Dixit had a quick and sudden death.

In short, Sai Baba's teaching was to have full and respectful faith in one's spiritual preceptor without showing unnecessary: cleverness or smartness. "Giving up multi-million smartness, repeat constantly 'Sai Sai' and your efforts will be successful. Do not suspect these words." (135)

— Chapter 10

"There is no need for possession of accomplishments nor for cleverness in six systems of Hindu philosophy. Only trust that spiritual preceptor is the only doer or saviour, who is required." (74)

— Chapter 19

15

'SABURI' (PATIENCE)

Out of two important points of Sai Baba's teachings, the second point is 'Patience' or 'Perseverence'. Patience means readiness to wait for the desired result as long as necessary. If there is full trust or faith in one's favourite or traditional deity or spiritual preceptor, patience comes automatically. Then, even if the results, in the beginning, are contrary to one's desires, one does not lose heart or faith in one's deity or preceptor. For instance in Chapter 11, Haji Sidiq Falke of Kalyan, after a pilgrimage to Mecca and Madina, had come to Shirdi for paying respects to Baba. Though the masjid was open to everybody, Falke was not allowed to climb its steps by Baba. Nine months thus passed but Falke did not give up. He requested Shama, Baba's favourite devotee, to mediate. Thereupon, Baba tested Falke's devotion by asking various questions and also by abusing him with harsh words. But Falke did not budge and as a result Baba was very pleased. After that Baba not only allowed him to enter the masjid but would invite him to have meals with him and also pay him cash.

Another example of patience is seen of Sapatnekar of Akkalkot in Chapter 48. How many times Sai Baba flouted his advances by shouting 'Get out'! But Sapatnekar had patience and at last Baba was pleased and blessed him with the desired boon for a son: Baba said, "Take this coconut and place it in the fold of your wife's saree, after which you can return happily giving up all worries." (166)

Similarly, look at Balasaheb Deo, the *Mamlatdar* of Dahanu, in Chapter 41. He had decided not to read the *Jnaneshwari* without clear orders to that effect from Baba. When Deo visited Shirdi, Baba accused him of stealing his rags and after a lot of abuses ran after him threatening to hit him also: "I shall hit you with an axe. I shall cut and kill you. Where will you run and go? I shall chase and kill you there." (118)

But Deo was not afraid: "Even after hearing such harsh abuses, Deo's mind did not waver. On the contrary, his heart was flooded with devotion and he considered those abuses as showers of soft and scented flowers." (153)

Afterwards, Baba demanded from Deo cash offerings repeatedly and Deo gave them without any hesitation. Naturally thereafter, Baba on his own, not only ordered Deo to read the *Jnaneshwari* but after a few days, by appearing before him in a dream, checked Deo's reading and gave further instructions in the matter.

Patience also means courage, resoluteness, perseverence and not to waver during calamities and misfortunes. Initially, Sai Baba used to remove devotees' calamities as per their requests but later on as the devotees progressed spiritually, he used to advise them to face these bravely since they were unavoidable being the results of the devotee's past actions: "They can be wiped out only by suffering them. This is the real truth during all the births and rebirths. To suffer their consequences is the only solution for getting rid of them." (82)

— *Chapter 13*

Once at Bombay, a steel cupboard fell on Kakasaheb Dixit's daughter Vatsala but nothing happened to her as Sai Baba saved her. But later on, while at Shirdi, she died and Kakasaheb was full of grief. So Baba picked up *Bhavarth Ramayana* of Eknath Maharaj and opening its page containing Rama's advice to Bali's wife Tara, after her husband's death, asked Kakasaheb to read it.

Similarly in Chapter 33, we see that when Nanasaheb Chandorkar's daughter Mainatai was having severe labour pains at Jamner in District Jalgaon, miles away from Shirdi, Sai Baba arranged for her safe delivery by urgently sending *udi* and *arati* with Ramgir Buwa of Shirdi. But later on, the child died and her husband had already passed away earlier. So she was now a childless widow in great misery. Consequently, when Nanasaheb, with all his family members, went to Shirdi, he was quite morose in front of Baba. Thereupon Baba said to him: "Nana! If you are coming here because of your worries for your son-in-law and grandchild, you are mistaken. Do not come to Me for this, because I do not control births and deaths of individuals. They are consequences of one's past actions. Even the all-powerful God who has created the world cannot make any changes in them. Do you think God can ask the Sun or the Moon to rise two hours or two days after the scheduled time or at different places than fixed? No! He will never do that because then there will be a great chaos."

Appa Kulkarni of Shirdi was charged with taking a bribe and the Deputy Collector ordered him to come to Ahmednagar for making a statement. Appa was naturally very scared and approached Sai Baba to save him. Sai Baba saved him but later on when Appa was suffering from cholera and started vomiting, his wife ran to Baba and requested him to save her husband. Baba said to her: "Do not weep. One who is born has to die some day." (156)

"When the coat becomes worn out or is no more liked by the owner, it is discarded." (159)

"This coat in the form of body, has been worn by the soul which is Lord Narayan Himself, who is imperishable, unbreakable and not admitting any alternative." (160)

"Therefore, do not by magic charms or incantations try to put any patches to the coat to keep it in use. Do not obstruct his path. Let him go to his destination." (161)

"Appa has made arrangements to change his *kafni* (long robe) ahead of Me. Do not come in his way." (162)

— *Chapter 31 of Arvachin Bhakta Leelamrit*
by Das Ganu Maharaj

We see that Gopal Ambadekar came under the bad influence of planets. His financial position worsened and calamities followed one after another. Ambadekar became disgusted with his family life and decided to go and commit suicide at Shirdi. "But Sai Baba thwarted his intention by making him read a suitable portion of Akkalkot Swami's life-history: "Thus he was advised that the allotted pleasures and pains in one's life have to be experienced." (135)

"Without suffering one's lot of diseases, leprosy, distresses and sicknesses and without experiencing one's allotments of pleasures and pains, how would suicide help?" (138)

"If the experience of allotted pleasure and pain is not complete, one has to be born again to complete that experience. Therefore bear your sufferings a little more and do not commit suicide." (136)

— *Chapter 26*

In short, Sai Baba used to constantly preach patience, ie, to wait for the desired result as long as necessary, not to lose one's balance of mind during calamities and to face them with fortitude: "Patience is the same as courage or fortitude. Do not ever lose it, because it alone will carry you across through difficulties and troubles." (53)

"A man's virility is this *saburi* or patience. It keeps off difficulties, mental restlessness and dejection. It removes all fears and apprehensions by averting all difficulties, by various devices and measures." (54)

"Patience is the mine of virtues or good qualities and the queen or king's good thoughts. She and faith are closely related sisters and are very intimately friendly." (56)

— Chapter 19

16

SERVICE TO THE DISTRESSED

From the very early days in Shirdi, Sai Baba used to serve the distressed and the poor. In the beginning, he used to go around Shirdi village and treat the sick persons: "In the beginning, He used to act as a physician and after examination used to prescribe medicines. His treatment was very effective and He became famous as a physician." (46)

"He did not charge any fees and brought health to the poor and helpless. With this effective treatment he became well known in that part of the country as a great physician." (47)

— *Chapter 7*

Sai Baba not only used to cure their diseases but sometimes drew them on his own body. Once Dadasaheb Khaparde's young son suffered from a very high fever while at Shirdi. At that time, Shirdi village had an epidemic of bubonic plague. Naturally the boy's mother got very worried and holding Baba's feet started requesting his permission to allow her to return to her native place, Amaravati. Thereupon Baba said in soft words: "The sky is full of clouds. It will rain soon and the crops will grow. Then the clouds will disappear and the sky will be clear." (106)

"Then, raising His *kafni* (long robe) up to the waist, He said, 'Why are you afraid?' and displayed to all those present four buboes which had appeared on His body." (107)

"There were four buboes of the size of a hen's egg all round and pointing at them He said, 'Look! How for your sake I have to suffer this burden of yours.' " (108)

— *Chapter 7*

Sai Baba not only used to cure the diseases of the distressed persons but also used to ward off their calamities, sometimes even at the risk of his own life. Once an ironsmith's wife was blowing the bellows. Being under the stress of her husband's anger, she forgot about her child in her arms. The restless child slipped from her arms and fell into the burning furnace. Sai Baba, being omniscient, learnt this and immediately thrust his hand in his own *Dhuni* (sacred fire kept continuously burning in Dwarkamai) and thus saved the child by pulling it out at that distant place. As a result, Sai Baba's hand was heavily burnt but he was hardly aware of it.

After some time, Sai Baba stopped giving medicines and started using the *udi* (holi ash from his *Dhuni*) for curing diseases. For instance, in Chapter 33, we see that Baba relieved Nanasaheb Chandoarkar's daughter Mainatai from labour pains, and in Chapter 34, he cured chronic bone-ulcer of a Malegaon doctor's nephew by prescribing *udi* only. This *udi* even today is found to be a most effective cure or a panacea for all diseases.

Sometimes, Sai Baba used to cure his devotees' diseases by using his superhuman powers. He cured Bhimaji Patil's tuberculosis by hitting him on his back with a cane and by rolling a stone up and down his chest in a dream (Chapter 13). Similarly he cured Dr Pillay's guniea-worms by making Abdul accidentally step on his outstretched leg (Chapter 34).

In the beginning, Sai Baba not only gave medicines to the sick persons, but would himself serve them in case there was nobody else to do so. Later on, when he grew old and there were many devotees to assist him, he used to get this service done through them. Once, a woman suffering from grave maladies came to Sai Baba who asked Bhima Bai to accommodate her in her house. So Bhima Bai said, "Baba, she is suffering from grave maladies. How can I accommodate her in my house?" Thereupon Baba said, "What if she is suffering from grave maladies? She is my sister—closest sister. Take her to your house." Naturally Bhima Bai took the woman to her house.

Similarly, when Balaji Patil Nevaskar requested Baba's permission to return to his village, Sai Baba said, "Dagdu Bhau is sick. Look after him and then go." Dagdu Bhau was suffering from black leprosy. Balaji Patil used to remove worms from his body, clean all excretions and bathe him clean. This process continued for sometime. Later on, Dagdu Bhau died and Baba permitted Balaji to return to his village. Similarly, in Chapter 32, a lady came to Kaka Kelkar and after seeing Baba wanted to keep a fast for three days. Baba advised her to give up her fast and feed herself and Kaka Kelkar's family sumptuously by cooking *puran polies* (wheat bread stuffed with sugar and ground pulses), since Kaka Kelkar's wife was not supposed to cook as she had her monthly menstruation period. Thus Sai Baba stressed to the lady the merits of assisting others in need over those of keeping religious fasts.

In our scriptures, the importance of feeding the poor and hungry is stressed repeatedly: "As amongst the six flavours, viz, sweet, sour, salty, pungent, astringent and bitter, the flavour of *varana* (a highly tasteful Maharastrian dish of pulse) is the best, the merit of feeding the hungry is the best." (21)

"At twelve o'clock in the noon, one gets uneasy due to hunger. One who realises this in the case of others also, is a virtuous person." (14)

"The householder should please a guest with meals, whether appearing at reasonable or unreasonable times. A householder who sends back a guest without offering him food is certainly inviting miserable life after death in the next birth." (17)

"One should feed those afflicted with grievous diseases/maladies, blind, lame, deaf and distressed persons first and one's own relatives afterwards." (23)

— *Chapter 23*

That is why Sai Baba, time and again, used to erect a big fireplace in the open space in front of Dwarkamai and himself cooked the food in a big vessel, distributing it to the poor and distressed persons. Similarly for those arriving from outstations to meet him, he used to arrange meals through the resident devotees of Shirdi either in their homes or by circulating a begging bowl for the purpose. Later, after 1910, plenty of dishes full of rich and varied food started pouring in as offerings to Baba and there was no need for Baba to cook himself.

Sai Baba's compassion was not just for human beings only but also for beasts, birds and small creatures like worms and ants also. Once a small dog, being bit by a mad dog, started chasing bigger dogs. The villagers with stick in their hands wanted to kill it. The poor little dog ran through the lanes and bylanes of the village and at last entering Dwarkamai hid behind Sai Baba sitting there. The villagers requested Baba to hand over the dog to

them as it was mad and they wanted to kill it. Baba said,
"Fools! Get away from here. Why should you kill this
dumb creature?" and thus saved the poor dog's life.

No wonder Hemadpant, the author of *Shri Sai
Satcharita,* in Chapter 23 says: "Sai Baba, the mother,
looked after those who had no owner or patron. Anything
rotten, fallen or wearied found repose in the Masjid." (110)

Sai Baba's getting his hands and feet massaged daily
with ghee (clarified butter) by the leper Bhagoji and getting
his outstretched legs pressed by his devotees (both males
and females) was only meant to benefit them and to teach
them the merits of serving others. Sai Baba did not require
such services nor did he want to show his greatness
thereby.

In short, in Sai Baba's teachings, service of the poor and
distressed had an important place. According to him, this
was a better method of worshipping God than keeping
religious fasts and vows. In this context, I am reminded of
Swami Vivekananda's following words:

"Do you like to see God
Face to Face
Here, in this world
with these eyes?
Serve a man in distress and See God
In his smiling Face."

17

READING OF BOOKS

Sai Baba had neither studied at any school nor at a teacher's house. He spoke rustic Marathi or Urdu language. He was never seen to be reading any Marathi or Sanskrit books nor the *Quran*. However, he not only knew the contents of these books, but remembered the words and their correct meanings also.

Once he said to Kakasaheb Dixit: "Read regularly *Vrindavan Pothi* (religious book)." Dixit could not understand anything. He showed a number of *pothies* to Baba but every time Baba said, "Not this," and asked for *Vrindavan Pothi* again. At last Dixit remembered *Eknathi Bhagavati*, a commentary on 11th chapter by Eknath Maharaj, and showed it to Baba, who not only said, "Yes! This is it!" but opening its 31st chapter, pointed at Ovi (Verse) no. 466 in which Eknath Maharaj himself had referred to his book as 'Vrindavan of 31st divisions'.

Similarly we know how in Chapter 39 of *Shri Sai Satcharita*, Sai Baba confused Nanasaheb Chandorkar, a Sanskrit scholar, by asking a number of questions regarding a Sanskrit verse from the *Bhagavad Gita*. When Nanasaheb could not give proper replies, Baba himself, like a learned scholar, explained its detailed and implied meaning with comments.

Thus Sai Baba realised the value of reading or listening to the reading of religious books and that is why he used to make some scholars and his learned devotees read such books in the open space in front of Dwarkamai or in some suitable places at Shirdi.

Sometimes Baba, looking at their capability, or on special occasions, insisted on his devotees reading a particular book. For instance, in Chapter 27 we see that Madhavrao Deshpande had borrowed *Eknathi Bhagavat* from Kaka Mahajani just to glance through it. Sai Baba, finding the book in Madhavrao's hand, asked for it, and afterwards, returning it to Madhavrao, said, "Keep it and read it." Madhavrao explained to Baba that the book did not belong to him, but Baba did not listen and insisted that Madhavrao should keep it.

Another similar example is in the same chapter about Bapu Saheb Jog, who went to Baba with a post-parcel just received. While bowing down to Baba, the parcel fell down at Baba's feet and Baba asked Jog what it was. When Jog opened the parcel in front of Baba, the contents turned out to be *Gita Rahasya* the commentary on the *Gita* by Lokmanya Tilak. Baba promptly picked up the book in his hand, turned its few pages and placing a rupee on it, returned it to Jog saying, "Read this carefully. It will do you good."

A third example is that of Kakasaheb Dixit. His daughter Vatsala had just expired at Shirdi and he was in a very dejected mood. Seeing this, Sai Baba picked up the *Bhavarth Ramayana* of Eknath Maharaj and holding it upside down and placing a finger in it opened it. On the opened page, there was an advice given by Shri Rama Prabhu to Tara after Bali's killing. Sai Baba asked Kakasaheb to read it.

If a devotee decided to read through a religious book in seven days as a vowed observance, Sai Baba would not only encourage him but guide him also. For instance, in Chapter 18, we see that when one Mr Sathe from Bombay came to Shirdi for peace of mind, being disgusted with his mundane life, and completed the seven days reading of the *Shri Guru Charitra*, Sai Baba appeared in his dream and: "Holding the book in His hand, Baba was explaining its meaning to Sathe." (44)

"Baba sitting Himself on the ground and making Sathe sit in front, was ready to narrate from the book." (45)

"Baba was reading through the book like a *Puranik* (expounder of ancient sacred poetical writings) and was narrating its meaning, and Sathe, like a good listener, was listening to the narration with a quiet mind and reverence." (46)

Sathe could not understand the meaning of the above dream and approached Sai Baba through Kakasaheb Dixit for clarification. Thereupon, "Baba ordered that one more reading of the book be carried out and the reader will be purified." (56)

Thus, by the above dream Sai Baba not only advised Sathe how to read a religious book but also put his advice into action by making Sathe read the book again.

In the case of devotees who could not carry out regular reading of a book, Sai Baba helped them by removing their difficulties. Balasaheb Deo, the *Mamlatdar* (officer in charge of a sub-division of a district) of *Thana* could not read the *Jnaneshwari* (Critical Marathi version of the *Bhagavad Gita*) regularly in spite of trying very hard. Therefore Deo decided not to read it unless Sai Baba himself ordered him to do so. Later, when he went to Shirdi, Sai Baba not only accused him of stealing his rag but in anger tried to hit him also. But all the time, Deo was quietly accepting all the accusations and abuses as bouquets. Actually Baba was removing Deo's obstacles in the reading of the *Jnaneshwari.* Then, Baba cooled down, called Deo nearer and told him to sit in Dixit Wada and read the *Jnaneshwari* daily and regularly. Also while reading, Baba advised Deo to explain the meaning to others. Thus, Baba not only fulfilled Deo's wish of reading the *Jnaneshwari* regularly but advised him how to read it also. Not only this, but after some time appearing in Deo's dream, Baba checked and corrected his method of reading also: "Baba said, 'You make too much haste while reading the book. Now sit near Me and let Me see how you read it.'" (164)

What great care and love for a devotee!

Generally it is believed that the highest and most excellent aim of man's life, ie, final beatitude or emancipation, is achieved by reading regularly religious books. In addition, if the same book is first offered to the preceptor and received back from him as a *prasad* (favour), the reading becomes more beneficial. There is some sense in this belief no doubt. But the reading must be with real devotion and faith. In Chapter 21, there is reference to Mr Patankar of Pune who had read all the *Vedas* and *Upanishads* (concluding part or essence of *Vedas*) with commentaries, but his restlessness had not ceased. So Patankar went to Sai Baba who jokingly told him how a trader collected nine balls of stools of his horse promptly in the fold of his cloth and achieved concentration of mind (by nine balls of stools Baba actually meant nine types of devotion): "Study of the *Vedas* and the *Upanishads,* continuous repetition of God's name, penance (religious austerity), religious vows and

practice of Yoga, discussion of the knowledge acquired of
Supreme Spirit—all these are useless without *bhakti*
(devotion)." (97)

Similarly, once on *Guru Purnima* Day (full-moon day
of *Ashadh* the 4th month of Hindu calendar when one's
Guru or spiritual preceptor is worshipped), Shri M.B.
Rege, a judge from Indore, saw many of Baba's devotees
carrying religious books, each to be presented to Baba and
getting it back with his blessings for reading. Rege had
brought no such book and so was feeling bad. Baba realised
this and so he said to Rege: "In these books, they want to
find *Bhrama* (God). There is however *Bharam* (whirl,
confusion or delusion) in these books. You are right. Do
not read books, but keep Me in your heart. If you unify
(harmonise) head and heart, that is enough."

—*Devotee's Experiences*
by H. H. Narsimha Swamiji Part I

Mere reading of books is not sufficient. Hemadpant
says: "What is the use of worshipping God without
devotion, and reading a book without understanding its
meaning?" (204)

— *Chapter 14*

"One should first read a book and then reflect on it.
Such repeated reading would result in intense
contemplation of its contents." (71)

"Mere reading of a book is not enough. It must result in
bringing its teachings into practice—otherwise such
reading would be like pouring water on an inverted vessel
(means such vessel will not collect any water). (72)

— *Chapter 21*

In this context, an experience is narrated by Deputy
Collector, Shri Vinayakrao Thakur, in Chapter 21. During

the probationary period while at *Vadgaon* (dist. Belgaum in Karnataka) with a land-measuring unit, he had an opportunity to visit a saintly person, who after blessing him presented him a book named *Vichar Sagar* by Nischaldas and said: "You can now depart. Note that your wishes will be fulfilled on reading this book. Later, during your tenure of service in the North, due to your great fortune, you will come across a great saint, who will guide you further and bring peace to your mind. He will then preach you firmly the knowledge of the Self." (33 to 35)

And really later, the Deputy Collector had an opportunity to go to Shirdi and meet Sai Baba who then said to him: "What Appa from Karnataka told you was like crossing a mountainous range riding on a male buffalo. But the passage here is not that easy. One has to labour hard here." (62)

Thus, for the sake of a devotee, the book *Nischaldas Vichar Sagar* was mentioned at Vadgaon and after its reading by the devotee, further action was advised at Shirdi.

In short, Sai Baba not only used to advise his devotees to read or hear the reading of good religious books but also removed any obstacles or difficulties during such readings, and guided them on how to read a book slowly, fully understanding its meaning and then by reflecting on its contents and bringing them in practice also. Then only would the reader get full benefit of his reading. Also in such readings one should have full faith and devotion, otherwise it would be nothing but sheer confusion of ideas and wastage of time.

18

DEVOTION TO GURU

The necessity of a *Sadguru* (spiritual guide and mentor) for knowing and realising Brahman (the Supreme Being) is considered essential in India since the ancient times of the *Vedas*. For instance, the *Mundoka Upanishad* says:

तद्विज्ञार्थ स गुरुमेवाभिगच्छेत्।
समित्पाणि : श्रोत्रियं ब्रह्मनिष्ठम् ।।9-2-92।।

– मुण्डकोपनिषद्

(For realising the Brahman—the Supreme Being, considered as the cause of the universe—one should approach a Guru, well-versed in the study of the *Vedas* and absorbed in the contemplation of the Supreme Being, carrying in hands small sticks of firewood for kindling sacrificial or sacred fire.)

In *Puranic* days also the following advice by Lord Krishna to Arjuna (the *Bhagavad Gita* and quoted in Chapter 33 of *Shri Sai Satcharita*) is well known to Sai devotees:

तद्विद्धि प्रणिपातेन परिप्रश्नेन सेवया।
उपदेश्यन्ते ज्ञानं ज्ञानिन : तत्वदर्शिन : ।।34।।

श्रीमद् भगवद्गीता अ. 4

(Remember! If you respectfully bow down to the wise and learned persons, question them again and again candidly and serve them sincerely, they will preach you the knowledge of the Brahman.)

In Chapter 39 of *Guru Charitra* by Saraswati Gangadhar, a Guru is described not only as Brahma, Vishnu and Mahesh (Creator, Preserver and Annihilator of the universe repectively) but as *Parabrahman* itself:

गुरुर्ब्रह्मा गुरुर्विष्णो गुरुर्देवो महेश्वर : ।
गुरु : साक्षात्परब्रह्मा तस्मै श्री गुरुवे नम : ।।३२।।

श्री गुरुचरित्र अ. 32

It further states that even *Devas* (superhuman beings), *Gandharvas* (celestial vocalists), *Pitaras* (deceased and deified ancestors of mankind inhabiting heavenly regions), *Rishis* (ascetics) and all *Sidhyas* (demi-gods or spirits inhabiting the regions between the earth and the Sun) cannot achieve liberation from births and deaths unless they serve their Guru.

न मुक्ता देवगन्धर्वा : पितरो यक्षकिन्नरा :।
ऋषयः सर्वसिध्दाश्चवगुरुसेवा पराङ् मुखा: ।।४७।।

Recently, about 400 to 700 years ago, Jnaneshwar in his *Jnaneshwari* and Eknath Maharaj in his *Eknathi Bhagavat* (both great Marathi saints) have reiterated the importance of a Guru again and again: "How to embrace the limitless? With what to whiten great lustre? How to hold the sky in its fist by a mosquito?" (74)

"But, there is one great prop for this, that is a favourable Guru, because of which, I am able to speak with confidence, says Jnaneshwar." (75)

— *Jnaneshwari, Chapter 1*

"Know that without a good Guru the realisation of Brahman as the cause and essence of the universe is not possible." (7)

"The eye may be beautiful and undamaged but without the help of the Sun it cannot see anything and stands still in the darkness." (8)

—Eknathi Bhagavat, Chapter 10

Sai Baba himself also has constantly praised the greatness of a *Guru*. He has also in simple words explained how to adore and serve a *Guru* by narrating his own experience, telling stories and sometimes even demonstrating examples of real *Guru bhakti* himself. In *Shri Sai Satcharita* therefore there are not only six chapters exclusively dealing with *Guru-seva* and *Guru-bhakti* but if from the whole of *Shri Sai Satcharita* various Ovies (verses) dealing on the subject are collected, they number 257 and become a Marathi version of *Guru Gita* in Sanskrit found in *Shri Guru Charitra*.

Once (Chapters 18 and 19) an old lady named Radhabai came to Shirdi with some persons from Sangamner (a *taluka* place in Pune district near Shirdi) and started fasting without food and water until Sai Baba favoured her with a secret incantation. But Sai Baba was not giving such incantation to anybody and even after three days of such fasting the old lady would not give up. Madhavrao was worried and requested Baba to call her and advise her.

Then Baba called her and said to her: "Look! My *Guru* was a great saint—an ocean of kindness. I served him until I was tired, but he would not give me the secret incantation." (47)

"In the beginning he demanded only two pices (old copper coins worth 64th part of a rupee) which I gave away instantly and requested for the incantation again." (48)

"The two pices were nothing but FAITH and PATIENCE. I gave those immediately. My Guru was then pleased with me immensely." (52)

"For twelve years I resided with my *Guru* who brought me up with great love and without any dearth of food and clothes." (61)

"How to describe that love? Looking at each other with eyes absorbed in meditation, we both were full of immense joy. I did not think of looking at anything else." (63)

"Day and night I used to look at my *Guru's* face. I had neither hunger nor thirst. My mind used to be restless without my Guru." (64)

"Without my *Guru,* I had nothing to meditate upon and nothing to look at. He was the only point of my attention. Indeed his doings were wonderful." (65)

"The mother tortoise feeds her young ones with her sight only. My *Guru's* method was also similar. He used to protect his children or devotees by look only." (68)

— *Chapter 19*

Thus, Sai Baba had prescribed a simpler method of meditating on one's *Guru* — with love and faith than by repeating an incantation or sacred magic formula, not only to Radhabai but to all of us. The same experience of Sai Baba has been described in Chapter 32.

"How sweet was my *Guru's* school! I forgot my attachment towards my parents. My chain of fascination for illusory objects was broken and I achieved liberation with ease." (76)

"All difficult bonds were loosened and impediments of active, worldly life were destroyed. I wished to put my hands round my *Guru's* neck and feast my eyes with his reflection." (77)

"Without my *Guru's* reflection in the eyes, I considered my eye as only a ball of flesh and preferred to be blind only. Such was my school." (78)

— *Chapter 32*

Similarly, even when the same *Guru* hung Sai Baba upside down in a well full of water, Sai Baba remained unconcerned and immensely happy. What great devotion to his *Guru!* No wonder that such disciples, in the words of Saint Tukaram, are raised by their *Gurus* to their own level without any delay.

Sai Baba, in addition, has time and again explained how to serve a *Guru* and what are the qualities of a good disciple:

1) Strict and Prompt Obedience of the Guru's Commands
However strange and difficult be the *Guru's* command, the disciple must carry it out promptly and without the slightest hesitation. Sometimes the *Guru* intentionally tries to test his disciple. For instance in Chapter 38, Sai Baba asked Dada Kelkar, a very orthodox brahmin, to purchase mutton from the market and that too on *Ekadashi* Day (11th day of the waxing and waning Moon which Hindus consider very holy), but as Dada Kelkar, like an obedient disciple set out, Sai Baba stopped him. Sai Baba asked Kakasaheb Dixit in Chapter 23, a religious and non-violent brahmin all his life, to kill a goat with a knife, but when he got ready to do so Sai Baba stopped him and jokingly said: "Kaka! Aren't you a brahmin ashamed to kill a poor goat?"

To this what Kakasaheb replied is worth noting: "Baba! Your nectar-like words are commands for us."

"We do not know any other religious practice. We are not ashamed to say that obedience of Guru's command is the only gist and the sacred scripture for us." (171)

"We are slaves of your commands. We will not consider whether the command is right or wrong. If necessary we will even sacrifice our lives in order to observe our *Guru's* command." (181)

Later, Hemadpant (the author of *Shri Sai Satcharita*), while defining the qualities of a good disciple, especially says: "He is the best disciple who knows the *Guru's* wishes without the *Guru* expressing them, and having known those wishes, starts acting on them without waiting for the *Guru's* commands."

2) Never Leave the Guru's Refuse or Shelter for That of Another Guru Howsoever Great
"Bear in mind this secret, that one should have firm faith in one's own *Guru* and nowhere else." (176)

"Even if the other person's *Guru* may have great fame and ours none, we should have faith in our own *Guru* only. This is the advice here." (178)

— *Chapter 12*

Sai Baba illustrated this time and again, by his own actions. For instance in Chapter 26, he asked Pant to return to his own *Guru*, and told Harishchandra Pitale and Gopal Ambedkar to continue the devotion to Swami Samarth of Akkalkot as per their family traditions.

3) Never Forget the Guru's advice
A *Guru* is aware of his disciple's capabilities and instructs him accordingly. Therefore, a disciple should only stick to instructions given by his *Guru* personally to him. Other saints' teachings, advice given by the *Guru* to other disciples, the *Guru's* own behaviour, whether observed or described, should not be followed.

"One should not disrespect other saints' words but (remember) who else can take better care than our own mother?" (117)

"If any other saint tells something, one should listen to his words, but one should stick to the advice given by one's own *Guru* only." (122)

"A doctor prescribes medicines and gives relevant instructions according to the diagnosis of the disease. Similarly, a *Sadguru* (spiritual guide and mentor) prescribes advice to his disciple who is sick of cares and pains, ills and turmoils, of worldly existence according to the level of his sickness." (113)

"You should not do anything because your *Guru* does so, but should follow only whatever has been told to you personally by him." (114)

"Always remember the *Guru's* words and meditate on them constantly. Remember always that those words only will lead you to final salvation." (115)

"When a *Guru* reads a religious book and explains the meaning of its contents, it is meant for the listeners only. As far as you are concerned, an advice given to you personally is to be followed—that is sacred scripture for you." (116)

— *Chapter 45*

4) Study and Work Hard

To achieve self-realisation, the disciple himself has to work hard. The *Guru* only shows the way: "Can anybody become a saint by wearing silk garments? He has to labour hard by grinding his bones and thinning down his blood." (79)

— *Chapter 4*

"One who craves for his highest and most excellent object, ie, final beatitude, must practise hard and take some risks also." (150)

— *Chapter 32*

"You start exercising and do not worry about milk. I would be there behind you with a bowl full of milk." (158)

"But if you say that I should do the exercising and you would swallow glasses of milk, well! I do not accept this. One must keenly pursue the accomplishment of one's work." (159)

— *Chapter 19*

Sai Baba's complaint used to be that nobody was prepared to work hard—everybody wanted instant result with ease: "My government tells me to take away the treasure but everybody wants Me only to collect it and give it to him. Nobody is paying attention to My call nor listens to My advice properly." (161)

"My treasure is full to the brim but nobody is bringing load-carts. I tell them to dig but nobody wants to dig nor try." (162)

"I say, dig that money and take away freely in load-carts. One who is the true son of his mother (means one who is prepared to work hard) only would take away that treasure." (163)

— *Chapter 32*

5) *Nine Qualities of a Disciple*

At the time of leaving this world, Sai Baba donated nine rupees to Laxmibai Shinde (Chapter 42). While explaining its implied meaning, Hemadpant, the author of *Shri Sai Satcharita*, has quoted nine qualities of a disciple mentioned by Lord Krishna to Udhava in the *Bhagavad Gita*. A disciple should remember them to obtain his *Guru's* favour: "A disciple should be humble (without arrogance), attentive, free from envy or jealousy, disinterested in worldly possessions, ever keen to serve his *Guru*, ever inquisitive of final beatitude or emancipation, of an

undisturbed mind and not indulging in calumny or
indulging in unnecessary talk in front of his *Guru*. With
these nine qualities he should try hard to please his *Guru
Maharaj.*" (125)

Quite correct! But will not these efforts of the disciple
be wasted if a proper *Guru* is not chosen? That is why
Hemadpant has in various places in *Shri Sai Satcharita*
defined the qualities of an ideal *Guru*: "Wise persons do not
consider him an ideal *Guru*, who is conversant with all six
shastras or works of religion (*Nyaya, Vaiseshika, Sankhya,
Yoga, Mimansa* and *Vedanta*) nor one who narrates and
explains *Vedanta*, ie, the *Upanishads* containing theological
part of the *Vedas.*" (3)

"Wise persons do not consider him an ideal *Guru*, who
controls his breath, who wears signs made with red-hot
stamping instruments of copper onto his body or who
delights listeners with discourses on Brahman (the Supreme
Reality) but is devoid of one's own experience." (5)

"He alone can be treated as an ideal *Guru* and he alone
has an authority to enlighten a disciple who has full
mastery over words as well as full experience in conveying
knowledge of Brahman." (8)

"He alone is an ideal Guru who never desires even in a
dream to get any service from his disciple but on the
contrary desires that his own body be of service to the
disciple somehow." (10)

"He alone is an ideal and beneficial Guru who is
without conceit that the Guru is the most superior and the
disciple is the most inferior." (11)

"He is the greatest *Guru* in the world who considers the
disciple also as altogether and absolute Brahman, loves him
as a son and does not expect any maintenance and
protection from the disciple." (12)

"That alone is the residence of an ideal *Guru*, which is the storehouse of great tranquillity, where there is no ego of learning and where great and small persons are considered equal." (13)

— *Chapter 48*

"He is the greatest *Guru* whose mind is full of compassion looking at the disciple's involvement in worldly affairs and is constantly worried as to how to get him rid of consciousness of being in the body." (58)

— *Chapter 10*

"There are numerous *Guru's* who catch hold of disciples forcibly and whisper to them sacred incantations by deceiving them financially." (61)

"One who teaches the disciple rules of religious behaviour but himself acts to the contrary, how can he relieve us from the cares and pains, toils and turmoils of worldly existence and chain of further births and deaths?" (62)

"There are two types of *Gurus*—permanent and transitory. Let us clarify to the listeners their respective goals to be accomplished." (65)

"To perfect their divine qualities and to purify the minds of disciples and to lead them to the path of self-realisation is the only gift of the transitory *Guru*." (66)

"On gaining contact with a permanent *Guru*, duality disappears and pantheism or non-duality appears. He then testifies the truth of the *Vedas* that Supreme Reality or Brahman is you." (67)

— *Chapter 10*

Sai Baba was not only an ideal *Guru* of the latter type but was a powerful *Guru* also: "There are numerous *Gurus* of worldly knowledge but one who gives self-realisation is the ideal *Guru*. However, one who takes you across the ocean of this worldly life is the powerful *Guru*—his greatness is unique and unsurpassable." (70)

— *Chapter 10*

And that is why Sai Baba could lead his devotees like Mhalsapati, Kakasaheb Dixit, Das Ganu Maharaj, Upasani Maharaj to the highest stages of spirituality. The most surprising thing is that in 1938, even after 20 years of his passing away, Sai Baba appeared at Karachi (now in Pakistan) before Shri Mota and explained to him some yogic exercises for achieving self-realisation; Shri Mota did achieve it finally on 29 March 1939 at Varanasi, on Ramanavami day.

Shri Mota is respected greatly in Gujarat State as a great saint. In his autobiography, he says: "Sai Baba gave final touches to my spiritual progress."

In short, as per the above instructions of Sai Baba, if a disciple serves an ideal *Guru* sincerely, his progress towards self-realisation would be certainly guaranteed. So great is the merit of a *Guru* and a disciple's devotion towards him. "One should dedicate with faith his body, mind and wealth also at the feet of an ideal Guru and spend all his life in the service of that Guru." (57)

"The *Guru's* name, the *Guru's* company, the *Guru's* favour, water in which Guru's feet have been washed and sacred incantation received from the *Guru* are very difficult to procure." (58)

"The above items have great powers. Staunch devotees have tested these. They will effortlessly push the devotees towards the gateway of liberation." (59)

— *Chapter 1*

19

ASTROLOGY

Nowadays, while arranging marriage, a lot of importance is being given to the consultation of horoscopes. Especially those from the bridegroom's side demand to see the horoscope and after consulting it refuse an otherwise very suitable girl on account of the planet Mercury located in a particular house or certain qualities not matching in the girl's horoscope. Similarly, our political leaders also, while filing their nomination papers for the elections or fixing the dates for the oath ceremonies of newly appointed ministers, consult astrologers for a suitable time and date.

Actually such great importance nowadays given to astrology is not correct. Firstly, compared to other sciences, not much study and research is being devoted to astrology and hence there is not much progress in that science recently. Moreover, the results of astrology have also a limit — any astrologer cannot deny that he can at the most predict 99 per cent only, the remaining one per cent being at the mercy of God Almighty, anything could happen.

Secondly, in this business of astrology, there are quite a number of swindlers of money. It is quite natural that everybody wants happiness and does not want dangers, pain, sickness or misfortunes, but is it ever possible to avoid them completely? Even then, every individual is constantly in search of ways and means to avoid them and astrologers take advantage of this weakness of theirs. By consulting the horoscopes or studying the lines on the palms of the individuals, the astrologers pinpoint the consultants' difficulties and sicknesses and gain their confidence. Afterwards, as a remedy they prescribe pacification of planets, performance of certain propitiations and repetition of certain incantations, and collect large sums of money.

If one believes in astrology and the methods of pacifications of planets, one should practise these methods himself as per instructions laid down in religious books, viz, hymns of praise to planet Saturn or Hanuman to get over seven year's inauspicious and calamitious influence of Saturn. By worship or religious service desired results could be achieved, but by merely dishing out cash without certainty of the necessary pacification rites or incantations performed by the astrologer correctly and thoroughly, the expected results cannot be guaranteed.

Another craze in this respect is the weekly prediction published in newspapers of individuals according to their Zodaic signs at the time of their births. Quite a number of persons believe them and become happy or sad by reading them. Actually if one makes comparisons, the prediction of the same Zodiac sign for the same period in two different newspapers many a time are quite contradictory. Any real astrologer will tell you that anybody's future cannot be correctly predicted only by noting his or her Zodiac sign. One has also to study other points such as the horoscope, other planets' influence and also horoscopes of nearest relatives such as that of wife or husband.

Until now we considered astrology from the point of logic. Now let us consider it philosophically. Really speaking, one has to suffer in this life whatever fate is destined as a result of good or bad deeds in one's former births. Even the liberated or self-realised person cannot avoid it. Astrology or palmistry can only give its indication. God has given to man the faculty of discrimination (to decide what is worthwhile and what is worthless), by using which he can change his destiny and if this is not possible, he can, at least by performing good deeds, lay the foundations of a better destiny in his future births. In this earthly life, both happiness and unhappiness are bound to be there. So to grieve over them or waste money and time over getting pacification of planets or incantations performed by astrologers or brahmins is not correct. One should, on the contrary, find a way out of them by using one's intellect, and if they are destined and unavailable, one should, as per the advice of Swami Samarth Ramdas, acquire fortitude to bear them willingly.

About astrology, Sai Baba's views are well known. Once a son of Raghunathrao Tendulkar from Bandra (now a suburb of Bombay city), studying in a medical college, was not appearing for his examination in spite of having studied hard, as an astrologer had told him that he would not pass in his examination. Later, when the boy's mother went to Shirdi and Baba inquired about her son, she told Baba that her son was not appearing for the examination that year on the advice of an astrologer.

"On hearing this Baba said, 'Tell him to listen to Me. Roll up the horoscope and appear for the examination with an undisturbed mind.' " (109)

"Do not be led away by somebody's advice. Do not consult the horoscope. Do not rely on palmistry, continue hard study." (110)

"Tell the boy that he will pass. Ask him to appear for the examination. Do not get disappointed. Have faith in Me." (111)

— *Chapter 29*

Then the mother returned to Bandra and told the son accordingly. The son also became enthusiastic and decided to appear for the examination. No doubt he passed both in the written as well as the oral examination successfully.

"Similarly, once an astrologer named Nana Dengle told Bapusaheb Butty that a particular day was inauspicious and alarming and asked him to be cautious. Consequently Bapusaheb was worried. Sai Baba, noticing this, said to him, "What does Nana say? Does he want to kill you? Why should we be afraid of anything? Let us see how he kills you." And on that very evening, when Bapusaheb had gone to the toilet, he found a snake there, but Bapusaheb was saved on account of Baba's grace.

A well-to-do businessman of Ahmednagar named Damuanna had two wives but no son. He had studied astrology and finding no chance of a male issue in his horoscope, was very dejected.

Sai Baba gave Damuanna four mangoes, asked him to give them to his younger wife to eat and assured that she would bear him four sons. Later, Baba's words were found correct and the predictions of astrology incorrect.

Once an Agnihotri brahmin (who maintains a perpetually sacred fire in the house) named Mulay Shastri from Nasik came to Shirdi along with Bapusaheb Butty's family. He was well-versed in astrology and in the interpretation of the spots, lines and other marks on the palm and sole of an individual. On seeing Baba, he was delighted and desired to examine divine signs (flag, thunderbolt, elephant goad, etc) on Baba's palms. He therefore moved further ahead and tried to request Baba to show his palm for studying. But Baba did not do so, but instead placed four plantains in his hands and sent him off.

Thus, time and again, Sai Baba proved the astrological predictions to be wrong and discouraged his devotees from consulting an astrologer or a palmist for prediction. He himself also did not permit any palmist to study his hand. Instead he advised his devotees to work hard for achieving success. At the same time, where the outcome was inevitable, he used to console them. When Kakasaheb Dixit was very grieved on account of his young daughter's death, Baba opened the *Bhavarth Ramayana,* and asked Kakasaheb to read the advice given by Shri Ram to Bali's wife Tara who was grieving over her husband's death. Similarly, when Bendre's eldest son was to die after four days, Baba advised him, "Be calm. Do not get upset."

According to me, for Sai Baba's devotees, Sai Baba's worship alone is pacification of planets, and Thursday is the auspicious day for any important work. In case due to some reason the work cannot be executed on a Thursday, it can be done on any other day by praying and remembering Baba at the time of the commencement of the work and applying his *udi,* I am sure the work will be successfully completed to ones satisfaction. But in case the results are not as per our expectations or one has to face any sad incident, one should learn to keep cool without losing faith in Baba believing that only Baba's wishes will have sway. Remember that Baba knows what and where our welfare is and he will always act for our ultimate good.

"Service to Baba will never be wasted. He will ultimately give you satisfaction of accomplishing your objects." (15)

— Chapter 45

20

VARIOUS RELIGIONS

Sai Baba's dress was that of a Mohammedan fakir. He lived in a dilapidated masjid (mosque) almost all his life and constantly repeated *Allah Malik hai* (God is the Master). He spoke in broken Urdu mixed with Marathi in vogue in the former Nizam State. His usual blessing too was *Allah tera Bhala Karega* (God will bless you).

At the same time, he did not mind his Hindu followers applying sandalpaste on his forehead and worshipping him in the masjid with *arati* accompanied by loud singing, clapping of hands and playing of musical instruments. He himself lit the fire (*Dhuni*) in the masjid and also kept a handmill along with a bag of wheat.

An Ramanavami day (birthday of Avatar Rama), He allowed a cradle to be hung in the open space in front of the masjid and took part in the birth celebrations with all gaiety and sprinkling of *gulal* (red powder), singing of *bhajans* and musical narration (*kirtan*) of the *Ramayana*. At the same time during Muharram, he allowed Muhammedans to keep the *Taziya* (*Tabut*) in front of the masjid, take out a 'Sandal procession' or to perform 'Namaz' whenever they wanted.

In short, Sai Baba treated Hindus as well as Muslims equally. In those days, these two communities were always quarrelling amongst each other and ridiculing each other's way of living and mode of religious worship. Naturally, when Sai Baba tolerated the actions of one community, the other community did not like it and sometimes expressed their dislike to Baba. But Baba gave tactful answers and silenced them.

For instance, Rohilla (a Muslim Jat from Rohilkhand), tall and well built and wearing a *kafni* (long robe), used to recite loudly and with great enthusiasm *Kalam* (verses from the Holy *Quran*) and shout *Allah ho Akbar* (God is great), day and night in front of Baba in the masjid. Most people in Shirdi were working in their fields by day and being tired, expected to sleep peacefully at night. But Rohilla's harsh cries and shouts did not allow them to sleep. So they (most of them Hindus) approached Baba and requested him to check the Rohilla and stop the nuisance. But Baba did not listen to their complaint and instead told them a jocular story that Rohilla had an immoral wife who did not like to live with him and shamelessly tried to come to Baba but hearing Rohilla's prayers she dare not enter and Baba was left in peace. Actually Rohilla had no wife and Baba was a celibate all his life. The story was just a joke to ward off the complaint.

Once a Muslim named Abdul Rangari asked Baba, "How is it that sandal is being pasted on your forehead? This is not our custom!" Thereupon, Baba replied, "*Jaisa Desh Vaisa Vesh* (When in Rome, do as the Romans do). The Hindus worship Me as their God. Why should I displease them? I allow them to do so. I Myself am a devotee of God."

But to carry on with this tolerance of other religions, Sai Baba sometimes had to use his yogic or divine power against his opponents. For instance, the tall and hefty Rohilla reciting the *Kalam* at night before Baba's masjid, was greatly puzzled about Baba. On one hand, Baba's vast knowledge and power made him think that Baba was *Parvardigar* (Almighty God on Earth). But Baba permitted himself to be worshipped at the masjid to the accompaniment of the noisy drums, pipes and the recital of *mantras,* and he allowed offerings to be made to Vitthal, Datta and other Hindu Gods. This, Rohilla, thought to be opposed to Islamic norms. He was shocked by Baba saying that all of them, ie, Vitthal, Datta, etc, were Allah. In accordance with the Islamic traditions that the destroyer of religion should be destroyed, he decided to kill Baba, who was in his view destroying Islamic religion by such irreligious practices. Therefore, one day he came behind Baba with an uplifted club in his hand and decided to end Baba and his heterodoxy with a single stroke. Baba, who of course, knew everything, knew his mind and power also. He suddenly turned and faced Rohilla and fixing him with a glance, touched his left wrist (the right one was held aloft with the cudgel). The effect was immediate. The man lost all his power to hold the cudgel and he fell down in a heap. Baba left him there and went away. For several minutes Rohilla lay there. When asked to get up by others, he declared that Baba had robbed him of all his powers. So he had to be lifted up.

Once a *Mamlatdar* came to Shirdi with a brahmin doctor from South Africa. The doctor said that his deity was Rama and that he would not bow before a Mohammedan, and hence he was unwilling to go to Shirdi. The *Mamlatdar* replied that nobody would press him to make a bow, nor would Baba ask him to do so. Therefore, he should come and give the pleasure of his company. Accordingly they came to Shirdi and went to the masjid for Baba's *darshan*. All were wonderstruck to see the doctor going ahead and saluting Baba. They asked him how he forgot his resolve and bowed before a Muslim. Then the doctor explained that he saw his beloved deity Rama on the seat and he, therefore, prostrated himself before Him. As he was saying this, he saw Sai Baba there again. Being dismayed, he said, "Is this a dream? How could he be a Mohammedan? He is great *Yoga-sampanna* (full of Yoga) *Avatar!*"

Thus Baba carried out his mission of uniting two quarrelling communities — Hindus and Muslims — sometimes by tact and sometimes by using his yogic or divine powers. He advised them thus, "Rama (the God of the Hindus) and Rahim (the God of the Mohammedans) are one and the same; there is not the slightest difference between them; then why should their devotees fall out and quarrel amongst themselves? You ignorant folks! Join hands and bring both communities together, act sanely and thus you will gain the object of national unity."

"If anyone does any evil unto you, do not retaliate. If you can do anything, do some good to others."

Sai Baba respected not only the religion of the Hindus and the Muslims equally but had a soft corner for Christianity and Zoroastrian religions also. When Chakra Narayan, a Christian, was appointed as Sub-Inspector of Rahata, some of Baba's devotees went to Baba and said, "Baba! We now have a Christian *Foujdar*." Baba's retort was, "What of that? He is my brother."

Similarly, during the Russo-Japanese war, Captain Jahangir Framji Daruwala, a Parsee, found that all his steamers except three were sunk by the enemy and that the rest of the steamers would soon meet the same fate. He took out Baba's photo from his pocket and with tears in his eyes, prayed to Baba to save him and his three ships. Baba, at once, appeared on the scene and towed all the sinking ships on to the bank. Immediately Daruwala offered his prayers. Baba bawled out '*Ha*' and then seated as He was in his usual place in the masjid. He had his *kafni* and headcloth completely drenched, dripping with water for more than half an hour, with the result that the masjid was transformed into a pool of water. The wonderstruck devotees had to remove the water and dry up Baba's clothes. On the third day, Baba received a telegram from Jahangir narrating how Baba had saved him and offering him a thousand thanks for the rescue of himself and the three steamers with passengers. Immediately on his return to India, he came to Shirdi to pay his respects to Baba and donated about Rs. 2,200/- for the repair of Masjid Sabha Mandap.

Sai Baba respected other religions and expected his followers/devotees also to do so. Once Baba came to know that Kakasaheb Dixit, one of his favourite devotees, had recently talked ill of Christ and Christianity at his lodging. So when he came and started massaging Baba's feet, Baba shouted, "Get away! Do not massage Me!" Dixit understood and repented. Baba then allowed him to massage his feet as usual.

Similarly, Baba did not like anybody changing his religion. Once *Bade* Baba (Fakir Baba) brought with him a recent Hindu convert to Islam (Ibrahim) to the masjid. Baba, slapping the convert on the cheek, retorted, "Ah! You have changed your father." Baba always advised everyone to stick to one's own religion, one's own deity of worship and one's own Guru (Preceptor). He used to say, 'Apna baap to apna baap' (nobody like one's own father)

In short, Sai Baba's mission was to convince everybody that all religions are nothing but different paths leading to the same goal, ie, realisation of God, and that the basic principles of all religions are the same. All beings are children of God—whether you call Him *Ishwar*, *Allah* or by any other name, and so His children should live in peace like brothers without fighting with each other on the basis of religion.

During his lifetime Baba ensured this in Shirdi with his tact, yogic or divine powers and timely *upadesh* (advise). The result was that whenever Baba sat in the masjid, both Hindus as well as Muslims gathered round him without any ill-feeling or caste pride; whenever Baba distributed food, both Hindus as well as Muslims partook of it without repulsion or hesitation, and whenever Baba moved out in a procession to *Chavadi* on alternate days, not only Hindus but Muslims also vied with each other for the honour of carrying various insignia of devotion, namely whiskers (*chamars*), umbrella (*chhatra*), etc. The main mass of devotees were Hindus and they carried on their worship of Baba at the masjid with rituals based on Pandharpur *Arati*. Their *bhajans* were full of allusions to Hindu mythology, but the Muslims who were present on such occasions enjoyed all this and freely partook of the offering distributed by the Hindu *bhaktas*. Similarly, whenever any Muslim devotees came to pay homage to Baba with flowers, sugar lumps, coconut and recited '*Fatia*' sometimes joined by Baba himself, the Hindu devotees sat quietly observing the rites in absolute silence, and respected and partook of the sugar lump as well as pieces of coconut with pleasure and joy. What a glorious harmony and brotherhood!

India needs the same harmony and brotherhood today very much in order to safeguard lives and property of ours, and to preserve the unity and integrity of our country.

Although the same is still seen at Shirdi where people from all communities—Hindus, Muslims, Sikhs, Parsees, Christians—gather together to offer their obeisance to Shri Sai Baba, it is required to be spread all over India. We, Sai Devotees, therefore, must make a beginning in earnest in this respect and set an example for others by precept and practice.

TEACHINGS SUMMARISED

Sai Baba's great devotee, Kakasaheb Dixit, has summarised Sai Baba's teachings in a few words in his preface to *Raghunath Savitri Sainath Bhajan Mala*, which is as follows:

"God is there and nobody is greater than Him. He pervades all living and animate and inanimate things, and still extends beyond. His play is unfathomable. He creates, He protects, He maintains and He also destroys. We should live as He keeps us. We should be satisfied in His wishes and not crave unnecessarily. Without His wish even a leaf does not move.

"Everyone should behave honestly (virtuously) and keep his conscience awake (to decide what is right and what is wrong). We should do our duty without accepting the pride of doership, which should be dedicated along with its fruit to God so that we will remain aloof without the action binding us."

"We should act lovingly towards all beings. We should not indulge in arguments. If anybody rebukes us we should bear it calmly. Words of rebuke do not cause holes in our bodies. We should not rival with others nor slander others. What others do we should not bother. Their actions with them and ours with us."

"Always be working. Do not sit idle. Remember God's name. Read religious books. No need to give up eating, drinking and going about altogether but they should be kept under control."

BIBLIOGRAPHY

1. Govind Raghunath Dabholkar alias Hemadpant, *Shri Sai Satcharita* in Marathi verse, 13th Edition, 1985.

2. Nagesh Vasudev Gunaji, *Shri Sai Satcharita*, 4th Edition, 1965.

3. H. H. Narsimha Swamiji, *Devotees' Experiences of Shri Sai Baba*, Akhanda Sainama Saptah Samithi, Hyderabad (A.P.), 1989.

4. H. H. Narsimha Swamiji, *Shri Saibaba's Charters and Sayings*, 7th edition 1975.

5. H. H. Narsimha Swamiji, *Life of Sai Baba*, Vol I (1974), II (1976), III (1978), IV (Birth Centenary).

6. Shirdi Diary of the Hon'ble Mr Khaparde

ELEVEN SOLEMN PROMISES AS PLEDGED BY BABA FOR MATERIAL SUCCESS, PROSPERITY & HAPPINESS

1. Whoever comes to my abode, their suffering will come to an end once and for all.

2. The helpless will experience plenty of joy, happiness and fulfilment as soon as they climb the steps of the Dwaraka Mayee.

3. I am ever vigilant to help and guide all those who come to me, who surrender to me and seek refuge in me.

4. There shall be no dearth of any kind in the houses of my devotees. I shall fulfil all their wishes.

5. If you look to me, I shall look to you and take care of all your needs.

6. If you seek my advice and help, it shall be given to you at once.

7. If you cast your burdens onto me, I shall surely take them on and relieve you of them.

8. I shall be ever active and vigorous even after casting away my body.

9. I shall respond and act in human form and continue to work for my devotees from my tomb.

10. My mortal remains will speak, execute and discharge all the needs of my devotees.

11. My tomb shall bless, speak and fulfil the innumerable needs of my devotees.